MARZIPAN
BANANAS

Blessings,
Ed

MARZIPAN BANANAS

And Other True Stories:
Footnotes on Life and Faith

Ed Ewart

ELM HILL

A Division of
HarperCollins Christian Publishing

www.elmhillbooks.com

MARZIPAN BANANAS
And Other True Stories: Footnotes on Life and Faith

Published in Nashville, Tennessee, by Elm Hill, an imprint of Thomas Nelson. Elm Hill and Thomas Nelson are registered trademarks of HarperCollins Christian Publishing, Inc.

Elm Hill titles may be purchased in bulk for educational, business, fund-raising, or sales promotional use. For information, please e-mail SpecialMarkets@ThomasNelson.com.

Library of Congress Cataloging-in-Publication Data

Library of Congress Control Number: 2018954520

ISBN 978-1-595559371 (Paperback)
ISBN 978-1-595559388 (Hardbound)
ISBN 978-1-595559234 (eBook)

To the special people in my life who gave me a new name, *Grandpa Ed!*

Royce, Bennett, Nathan, Hallie, Eric, Jake, Ian, Jeremy, Tyler, Ryan, Molly, Charlie, Zachary, Max, Caroline, and Paige.

TABLE OF CONTENTS

ACKNOWLEDGMENTS

I'm deeply grateful to God for seasoning my life through my shortcomings, mistakes, and failures. More than through outward successes and accomplishments, I seem to learn the most important lessons by falling on my face. As any toddler knows, learning to walk is well worth a few bruises; as every Christian believes, *"All things work together for good [even our tumbles] for those who love God, who are called according to his purpose."* (Romans 8:28)

I am grateful to all the people who have been part of my story. I'm glad I haven't lived like a solitary fish in a bowl; I have enjoyed the company of vast schools of people who have traveled with me (or gone before me) and enriched the journey.

I owe the inspiration for "One-Eyed Teddy" to a sermon I heard forty years ago about a rag doll. It was preached by Ian Pitt-Watson, who was then professor of preaching at Fuller Theological Seminary in Pasadena, California. To my knowledge he never formally published the sermon but his imagery *inked* its way into me. I came to realize that my *One-Eyed Teddy* was very much like his daughter's rag doll. A recording of his sermon is available through www.preachingtoday.com

(a resource of Christianity Today) under the title "Knowing and Loving God."

Most especially I am grateful to my treasured longtime friends and thoughtful proofreaders, Mike and Lynne Barrette. Mike is also the gifted cameraman who embellished some of these old memories with his photographic and processing skills. (You can see Mike's incredible photographic work at *michaelbarrette.myportfolio.com*.) I also deeply appreciate the generous editorial counsel of my friend and member of Mount of Olives Church, Andrea Nolen. These three dedicated friends volunteered untold hours of their time to help me pass these stories on. Any errors in this manuscript are the result of my final edits, not theirs!

I'm also deeply grateful for my granddaughter, Hallie, whose creative mind and artful hand provided the wonderful illustrations that help to tell these stories. (Inquiries regarding Hallie's artwork can be directed to hmbillustrations@gmail.com.)

Finally, my unparalleled appreciation and love belongs to my constant helper, cheerleader, and wife, who I sometimes call *Grandma Linda* and who often corrects me, "I'm not YOUR grandma!"

AUTHOR'S NOTE

This book is dedicated to the special people in my life who call me *Grandpa Ed*. It is also written in response to some other gracious people who have listened to my stories and encouraged me to write them down. Together they have reminded me that we never outgrow our appreciation for a good story, especially if it's true!

All of these stories are true in three important ways.

First, they happened just as I have written them. Telling the truth to your grandchildren is important, especially when you are reporting about the events of your life. While I have changed some of the names, the people and the events are as accurate in detail as my memory permits. If you doubt some of these things, remember the old saying, *Truth is stranger than fiction.*[1]

Second, these stories are true because each of these *snapshots* taught me something worth remembering over a lifetime! In every case they recall *teachable moments* that tattooed themselves into me, got under my skin, and have colored who I am today.

Most importantly, these stories are true because they resonate with the oldest and truest stories I know. Thousands of years ago, some grandpas began writing down their true stories of life and faith for their grandchildren. Their Bible stories are older and better than my stories, but mine are a kind of modern-day footnote to theirs. In spite of the thousands of years between us, the authors of Scripture and I believe that God speaks to us in our daily experiences. It is this grandfather's privilege and joy to learn from what He has said and to pass it on.

So keep your eyes open Royce, Bennett, Nathan, Hallie, Eric, Jake, Ian, Jeremy, Tyler, Ryan, Molly, Charlie*, Zachary, Max, Caroline, and Paige. God is still writing and by the time you are my age, you too, will have some great stories to tell.

Love,

Grandpa Ed

*Charlie's eyes are already opened wide and his stories are beyond our wildest dreams!

1

MARZIPAN BANANAS

But the serpent said to the woman, "You will not die; for God knows that when you eat of it your eyes will be opened, and you will be like God, knowing good and evil."

So when the woman saw that the tree was good for food, and that it was a delight to the eyes, and that the tree was to be desired to make one wise, she took of its fruit and ate; and she also gave some to her husband, who was with her, and he ate.

Then the eyes of both were opened, and they knew that they were naked....

GENESIS 3:4-7A

When I was growing up, our Christmas tree never came down until New Year's Day. I just assumed that the season of candles, carols, and gifts wasn't over until the final tick of the clock at the Rose Bowl game. If a Western PAC team won, it was celebrated with a final fist pump to the season of lights. If a team east of the Rockies won, taking down the tree felt like you were wrapping Christmas in linens and burying it in the Coliseum for another year. For a child growing up in Southern California, the week following Christmas strangely connected Bethlehem and Pasadena.

It was the early 1950s and I was a lad of eight. I'd never been to the Rose Parade and that year my two favorite TV celebrities, ventriloquist *Buffalo Bob* and his wooden dummy *Howdy Doody*, were to be in the Pasadena parade. My parents made arrangements to spend New Year's Eve at Uncle John and Aunt Isabel's home just a block from the parade route on Colorado Boulevard.

Uncle John and Aunt Isabel were in their seventies. Their house was dim and museumlike. It never smelled like *Spic and Span*® the way ours did after my mom's frequent cleanings. Their living room was furnished with an emerald-green sofa and two matching chairs. The rough dark fabric was stitched in a floral relief pattern. Far from the feel of soft green leaves, this industrial-grade fabric felt like sandpaper against your skin—no wonder those couches lasted forever!

The familiar aromas of the small house wafted through the various rooms and fermented in that *green garden of fabric*: Aunt Isabel's lilac-scented perfume, Uncle John's cherry-blend tobacco, the fragrance of lemon furniture polish, the smell of countless chicken dinners, and of course, the scent of pine needles from the Christmas tree standing in the corner.

New Year's was the culmination of the season of surprises, and

Aunt Isabel loved surprises. After a polite welcome, she went over to the pile of opened presents beneath the Christmas tree. One present remained unopened. She pulled it from beneath the tree. Handing it to me, I pealed the paper wrapping off to discover a box with a picture of dancing dogs in ballet tutus on it. There was also a little boy in a red shirt beating on a blue drum. I lifted the lid and was amazed at what I saw.

Inside the box was a harvest of the tiniest fruit I had ever seen. There, individually cupped in ruffled paper collars, were *red* apples and *orange* oranges, *purple* plums—and tiny *yellow* bananas. In bold black letters the label on the box read, "Marzipan Fruities."

"What's M-A-R-Z-I-P-A-N?" I asked Aunt Isabel.

"A delicious confection of almond paste, sugar, and egg whites," she read from the box.

"Oh," I said, smiling, as if I knew what almond paste was.

Knowing my love of candy, my mother's watchful eyes were on the box as well.

"You may have one," she said, "but tomorrow is a big day, so one will be enough." She waited for eye contact.

"Do you understand me, Eddie?"

"Yes, Mother." I understood perfectly!

Of course, I was thinking to myself, *How silly of Mother to think that eating too many of these tiny morsels could make a person sick.* My parents said so many foolish things when I was young; things that were obviously untrue:

"Don't pick at that scab; it will never heal."

"If you cross your eyes, they'll get stuck and you'll be cross-eyed forever."

"Don't tease the cat; it makes her nervous."

"Marzipan will make you sick!"

I was eight years old—I knew better than to believe all of that foolishness!

I saw my uncle sneak a second piece of candy; I think it was a pinkish peach. I watched closely as he savored it. He stopped chewing as he noticed my stare. I guess he didn't want me to suffer while he enjoyed himself.

Why is it that adults think candy will make children sick when they themselves eat all they want when the children are out of sight? I watched without his awareness as he swallowed his second piece. He still seemed perfectly healthy. My entire family was older than me, but I knew they were less knowledgeable than I was about the effects of Marzipan. I reasoned that what was good for Uncle John would be just as good for me.

The tiny sample I had been given, a banana, was delicious! How could more of this delight make me sick? Even if I did start to get sick—all I'd have to do is just stop eating it! Besides, this candy looked like produce. It was less like eating candy and more like eating fruit, or even vegetables. What kid ever got sick from eating too many fruits and vegetables? Mom's warning was like saying: *If you eat all your apples and carrots you'll get sick*! *Son, take it easy on the carrots—not too many!*

Sure, maybe if you ate a ton of marzipan, you'd get sick. I could understand that, but these little yellow bananas were so small.

The adults resumed their conversation, and I began playing with the electric train under the Christmas tree. They were busy in conversation, so they didn't see me open the colorful box at the base of the tree again. I quickly picked all the randomly placed bananas from each layer of the box and removed their telltale paper collars. I figured that if there were no bananas AND no paper collars remaining in the box, no one would even notice that they'd been harvested. I stuffed the plucked fruit into my pockets, blowing the train whistle now and then to distract from my real agenda.

I was pretty sure I knew the real reason Mother delighted in denying me marzipan. It was because my parents loved to say, "No." As an eight-year-old, I knew that whenever a parent can say "No," they feel powerful! Just saying "No" to a kid gives a parent a sense of purpose. Show me a mother who says "Yes" to a kid and I'll show you a parent who feels weak and useless. A good stern, "No, and that's final," makes a parent feel like God put them here for a reason! Kids don't carry the Ten Commandments around with them on those tablets, so God gave kids parents to say "Thou shalt NOT."[1] If everything was "Yes," I reasoned, parents would be unnecessary. If everything was "Yes," kids wouldn't even have to ask. But as it is, every kid knows the drill.

Dad, could I....

No, absolutely not! Your chores aren't done and I'll bet you're not done with your homework! When you graduate from high school, get a job and have a family, then you can have fun like me. Until then, the answer is NO!

That's just how parents are; they figure saying "No" is a way to stay in charge so they put "No" on autopilot. What eight-year-old truly believes their parents have ever once had a good reason for saying "No"?

Of course that was the best reason Mom could have had for saying "No." She wanted to play God and limit my fun. But then I reasoned— maybe the real reason was that the adults wanted ALL the marzipan for themselves! I thought to myself, *They'll wait until I go to bed and when I am sound asleep, they'll have a marzipan banquet. They'll gorge themselves with MY CANDY, like bullies stealing lunch on the playground, and in the morning when I wake hungering for one tiny piece, they'll tell me it has vanished or that the marzipan is just for adults—like all the best stuff in life!* Power makes adults so stingy.

Perhaps the adults would even try hoping that I would forget about marzipan by putting it on a high shelf out of my sight *for my own good,* saying it was for later, but I would smell the faint scent of marzipan on their breath in the morning and I would know the truth! As we all once knew—parents cannot always be trusted and they have little understanding of how smart their children are!

As I lay in the dark that night, I reached into my pants pockets nearby and snacked over-and-over on the succulent sweets. I never gobbled them to gorge myself. I carefully savored each morsel like a prize-winning fruit in a county fair. I rolled the delicate pieces over and over in my mouth, enjoying the syrupy finish as the flavor poured over my tongue. I thought to myself, *If you just wolfed them down like a glutton who didn't appreciate almond paste and egg whites maybe you could get sick—but enjoying a little fruit at bedtime couldn't harm anyone.* How could anything that looked so good, smelled so sweet, and tasted so delightful be bad for a person? In fact, I reasoned it's probably good for you to have a little nibble of fruit before sleep. Why, Mom herself used to put bananas on top of an evening bowl of cereal. How could this possibly be any different (EXCEPT, there was no milk, or cereal, or real bananas—otherwise, it was exactly the same)!

I woke up New Year's morning feeling a little woozy. *No problem, a little breakfast will clear this up*, I thought. I popped a few more candies into my mouth. Strangely, they did not taste as good as they had the night before.

We bundled up in the crisp morning air and began our short hike to the parade. As is often the case in Southern California, my sweater became nothing but a burden after 8:00 AM. When the warm sun rose and the parade began, I felt as though I was smothering in my sweater. Curiously, I didn't seem to have the energy to take it off.

It's amazing what happens to an eight-year-old boy who stands sweater-bound in the sun for a three-hour parade with less than the usual amount of sleep and quarter of a pound of almond paste and egg whites in his stomach. My head began to ache. My palms were sweaty. My stomach felt like the electric train under the Christmas tree was running circles inside it.

I took my sweater off, but it was too late. I was sick! I had no interest in the parade. If Buffalo Bob and Howdy Doody rolled by, they were completely upstaged by the rolling that was happening in my stomach. I was deathly ill, but I couldn't admit it.

Mom spotted my pale stupor and knew immediately something was wrong. We left the parade early. I staggered and bumped my way through the crowd on our way back to the house; Mom no doubt wondered what it could be ... *a flu bug ... the onset of measles ... too much excitement*? But I knew what it was. The churning deep within my inmost being told me it was MARZIPAN POISONING!

When we finally got back to Uncle John's house, Mother gently laid me on the dark-green sofa. Now the ripe essence of lilac, cherry, lemon, chicken, and white pine began to heavily *season* the already potent gastric curse. I lay there motionless—trying not to breathe—staring at my electric train on the floor—surrounded by *toxic fumes*.

Soon after, the others returned telling of the wonders of the parade which I had totally missed. Sympathetically they tried to interest me in the football game but by now my eyes were rolling back in my head as I silently prayed, "Dear God, take me home!"

It was about that time that Uncle John decided to indulge in a little snack before *kickoff.*

He plucked the box of candy from beneath the Christmas tree and generously passed it around to the others. As it passed by, I could see the hideous fruit staring up at me with their disgusting little shapes and grotesque colors. The smell of marzipan filled my nostrils. I could feel the almond paste and egg whites within me, churning for *liberation*.

"Hey," Uncle John said, "where're all the bananas?"

They arrived with a flourish—like a real life-size train bursting through the living room—I sounded two short warning blows before delivering one long and decisive blast. Innocent bystanders scurried for cover. My mother bolted toward the arriving disaster, hanky in hand.

A new fragrance now dominated the bouquet of perfumes that filled the house—*forbidden fruit*! There it was, in all its naked splendor. There I was, sick as sin with nowhere to hide. Mom had been right all along.

I don't remember being punished. I think Mom knew I'd already experienced divine retribution and there was no need to pile on more. She lovingly administered the antidote, a bowl of good-tasting chicken soup.

That New Year's Day, planned as a special experience for me decades ago, instead ruined my taste for marzipan for life. The mere thought of marzipan (and certainly the smell of it) to this day gives me a sour stomach.

Surprisingly, I'm not altogether cured from overindulgence. Old as I am, I'm still tempted from time to time to devour too much of something thinking that sound warnings are irrelevant. What I have learned is that often, what is secretly indulged in as, "*a delight to the eyes ... to make one wise ...*"² often turns out to be not much more than an excess of almond paste and egg whites in clever disguise.

Thank God for a merciful mother and chicken soup!

2

ONE-EYED TEDDY

For while we were still weak, at the right time Christ died for the ungodly…

But God proves his love for us in that while we still were sinners Christ died for us.

Romans 5:6–8

One-Eyed Teddy is not your average bear. In fact, One-Eyed Teddy is far less than average! Usually teddy bears are adorable, soft, and cuddly. One-Eyed Teddy is really none of the above. One-Eyed Teddy is too threadbare to be adorable. His fur looks like the moths have been at him for many winters. He has only one eye and nothing but a patch of fuzz where the other one should be. His fur has grown a little too rough over the years for kids to find him huggable. And—I hate to admit it—but if you put your nose right up to him, he smells a little musty. One-Eyed Teddy is pushing seventy-five now and there's no question that his days as a cub are long gone, but there is a special place for him in my study—and in my heart.

I can't remember if he ever looked any different from the way he looks today—although maybe that's just love talking. When my aunt Ann gave him to me, I'm sure he had two eyes and a fuzzy-feel. I was told that she laid him in my crib as I slept—from the looks of him—he received a bear hug from me every time I opened my eyes from that day on.

I'm sure there was a time when I was young when those stitches from his neck to his bellybutton (that now resemble open-heart surgery) were just fluffy fur, when that bare patch on his side and his half-smile grin were more baby-friendly. There must have been a time when both his ears stood up straight. The truth is I don't remember him any other way than he looks today with his nose a little off center, as if he had been a boxing bear in his youth.

Today he sits in the corner of my study at home, which has become a museum of memories. To look at him now you'd think my aunt got a deal at a garage sale, or more likely rescued him from a trash can. But I'm sure that on his day of creation he was *"very good ..."*[1] and well suited to rule the toy box. Spending twenty years in secret hibernation in the attic of my home in Northern California probably further contributed to his decaying condition.

The truth is, as a child, it was *love at first sight* between me and Teddy, and he is no less lovable to me today. Teddy has taught me that *some things are loved because they have value—but some things have value because they are loved.*

I loved my first car because it was a stick shift, *three on the tree,* with a red racing stripe and red upholstery. I got a lot of high school girls to ride in my car. Other guys in my high school thought that was pretty valuable too.

My childhood love for Teddy was different. There were lots of other toys but I invested my affection in him. My love for One-Eyed Teddy poured value into him. I loved my first car, and so did my buddies, because it was valuable. I loved Teddy for no reason apparent to others. I just loved him. I'm guessing the bond began the moment I opened my eyes in my crib and cuddled him to myself the very first time.

Who knows what makes a thing lovable to one person and not to another? My mother's parents didn't care for my dad much when she first started dating him. He was an orphan with no visible means of support. In fact, the first time she saw him she laughed out loud. She was watching him from her living room window. She saw him walking on the other side of the street on a cold Pennsylvania day. He was strolling down the street in the middle of winter without a hat on. He had rather large ears and looked kind of like the dancing movie star Fred Astaire (not plain, but not particularly handsome).

She said to herself, "What a silly-looking young man to be walking down the street in the snow without a hat." The thing is, without a hat, she saw him very clearly; that first vision seemed to stick with her for a lifetime. Whenever we talked about him after he passed, she would delight in retelling one particular story again and again. She described him coming home from the nightlife in town late on Saturday nights and she would watch for him and meet him on the back porch stairs. Then they would get to cuddling and kissing and finally (lost in her memories) my ninety-year-old mother would breathe a long deep sigh and say—"Oh my!"

Mom never tired of telling that story. I think she enjoyed reliving it as she told it. That sigh would have filled a hot air balloon!—and I do mean *HOT*!

Sometimes love can't be explained. What is it that makes a person attractive to one person and not to another? Whatever it is, Dad got under Mom's skin.

Dad loved Mom plenty too. He loved to make her laugh, he loved to tease her. Countless times I watched her occasional frustrations with him melt into laughter at his antics. It was his secret weapon and it nearly always worked. He felt so fortunate to have a job and to be able to provide for us; to him, nothing else in life was worth quibbling about.

My love for One-Eyed Teddy was like that. There were lots of other toys, even other teddy bears to choose from in my toy box, but nothing else had quite the same value. I went to sleep with him and woke up with him. He was the one I spilled cereal on, the one I dragged to the doctor's office with me when I was having my arm cast removed. He was the one that made me smile.

One summer my mom and I rode the Santa Fe Railroad's El Capitan back East. Of course I took One-Eyed Teddy and all the passengers got to know the three of us pretty well. We'd meet people as we made our way from our tiny reserved suite to the dining car.

Once I lost Teddy. I cried as I thought he was gone forever. Nothing could console me. We looked everywhere on the train before the conductor happily reunited us. He said he found Teddy sitting on a table in the dining car just after breakfast. He joked that he was staring at a jar of honey.

I found out much later in life that during our eight weeks in Pennsylvania, my mother was considering whether she should be looking for another husband. It seems my Baptist-born-and-bred mother had smelled beer on my father's breath. He had broken the promise he made on their wedding day never to drink alcohol again. While she dearly loved him, she decided to give him two months to think things over. I wonder now whether as a youngster I had some inkling that things were amiss and whether One-Eyed Teddy became all the more important to me over that time when I was no doubt missing Dad.

In the long run, One-Eyed Teddy was returned from the dining car, and mother and I returned to California and to Dad. Teddy promised me no longer to be lured by honey, and Dad made a similar promise to Mom about hops. The whole family was reunited. To my knowledge, Dad never broke his second promise.

I can't remember when One-Eyed Teddy went missing the second time. I just know that one day during an attic cleaning, he was discovered and thoughtfully delivered back to my arms for safekeeping. For years I placed him on the grandchildren's toy shelves in our den. After they hugged and greeted us, they'd go straight for the toy shelves. It's funny—I don't remember a single time when one of them picked Teddy up and cuddled him. I do remember some of our adult children, now parents, suggesting that if we were going to keep him on the toy shelf, we might consider having him "fumigated." Instead, I just moved him upstairs to my study where I wink at him now and then and he winks back because that's really all a One-Eyed Teddy can do.

Teddy never did anything to earn my love except be there! His value was not in anything he initiated but regardless, I poured my love into him—that's why he was valuable.

When Paul wrote, *"But God proves his love for us in that while we still were sinners Christ died for us…"*[2] he had the choice of several Greek words that all carry different shades of meaning for "love." He chose the one that is rarely mentioned outside of the Bible. He chose the Greek word "agape." You see, the other words better define the things that are loved because they give something valuable in return; agape defines the kind of love that makes a thing valuable just because it is loved.

The Bible tells us we are all One-Eyed Teddies. Many of us have scars in hidden places that feel as prominent as the stitches on Teddy's chest. Some of us feel a little shabby inside for the things we've done—or even for some terrible thing that happened to us that we can't seem to forget. A lot of people fear that deep down they are worn, musty, and unlovable. Some have grown so calloused and coarse that they are uncomfortable with hugs. It's as though they fear that if folks got close enough to see them clearly, they wouldn't want to embrace them.

In the end, these things do not get in God's way; he loves us because he has always loved us from the first time he laid eyes on us. He loves us in spite of our scars and self-inflicted shabbiness. He loves us regardless of our half-sightedness. The mustiness and the scuffing only make it clear to him that we are the ones he has loved from the start.

The only thing that really makes something or someone *perfectly lovable* is *LOVE*! The deepest love can't be explained; it can only be embraced. A new mother does not scan the hospital nursery for an attractive baby; she looks for her own!

God loves you just the way you are. You are enough. You have always been enough. You will always be enough. *You are not loved because you are valuable. You are valuable because you are loved!*

14

3

PACKARDS AND POP GUNS

Thy eyes beheld my unformed substance; in thy book were written, every one of them, the days that were formed for me, when as yet there was none of them.

How precious to me are thy thoughts, O God! How vast is the sum of them!

If I would count them, they are more than the sand.

When I awake I am still with Thee.

PSALM 139:16–18 RSV

You and I have overcome incredible odds just to be "talking" to one another right now!

The instant we were given life, the chances of you being YOU and me being ME were three hundred million to one. Two million, nine hundred ninety-nine thousand, nine hundred and ninety-nine other sperm cells fought hard for dominance the moment you were conceived. And YOU won!

The sperm that fertilized your mother's egg was a gold medal winner of much greater than Olympic proportion. Before your first breath, you had already conquered odds infinitely beyond winning the lottery. The average person is far more likely to be struck by lightning or attacked by a shark than you were likely to be the unique and distinct person that makes you YOU!

Of course now that you are older than a fertilized egg, you know that it's not just a lot of hard work that got you here. It's more like a gift! Champion that you are, you didn't really get here on your own; and if you're like me, you've *pressed your luck* in a few risky situations since the day you were born.

When I was five I discovered a rusty razor blade in our back alley. I energetically began using it to cut down a eucalyptus tree. As a result I have a scar on the back of my hand that reminds me that I could have accidentally slit my wrist instead!

Once, at the age of seven, I pinned a bath towel around my neck and jumped off the garage roof in an attempt to fly like *Superman*. All I received for leaping off a tall building with a single bound was a single "thud"—and a sling for my sprained shoulder.

I nearly drowned when I was eighteen while body surfing at "The Wedge" in Newport Beach.

In my twenties I almost fell off the boarding ramp of a ferryboat into the churning propeller below. I was trying to board after the *all clear* buzzer while on crutches in a full leg cast. The hinged boarding ramp fell away behind me just as I got my good leg on the deck. The deckhand just looked at me and shook his head in disbelief—and relief.

Even as an adult I've tempted fate by trimming tall trees with a chain saw. I've tumbled over the handlebars of my bicycle twice, miraculously receiving only one broken collarbone. Once I posed for a picture an inch from the end of the granite *diving board* on top of Half Dome 4,800 feet above Yosemite Valley. On top of all this, I've even survived eating my own bachelor cooking—with only temporary ill effects.

Being born is a statistically unlikely gift, staying alive for many of us is also an unexplainable mercy. We who have been so fortunate as to survive three hundred million to one odds plus a few more just to stay alive should know that EVERY DAY IS A GIFT. We should be *high-fiving* perfect strangers on the street just because anyone who was born and is still here is a member of a very privileged team.

I came along late in life for my mother and father. Mom was almost forty years old when she had me. I was the only child they NEVER expected to have. They told me that they tried for years and then when they finally gave up, I happened. Before I was even born, they loved me deeply. They named me Ruth, which they promptly changed to Edward after my arrival.

I was given a lot of attention as a child. My mother quit teaching school from the time I was born until I was in middle school so she could be right there with me as I grew.

There was a lot of love in our home. I remember sitting on my mom's lap in the rocking chair listening to the radio at night. I remember my father doing acrobatics with me on the living room carpet. He would lie on his back on the floor and I would put my feet in his hands and stand stiff as a board as his strong arms lifted me upright into the air—no wonder I grew up thinking risk-taking was fun.

These special family moments, by contrast, must have made what happened one summer afternoon, when I was four, an absolute nightmare for my mother.

Cheryl and Renee Swan lived three houses up the block from us. They were older and had permission to travel to the "far country" of my home. Finally, after several months, my cautious mother allowed me to play now and then in their front yard. On these privileged occasions, Mother would be out working on some project in our front yard so she could keep a watchful eye on me from a distance.

It was about four o'clock on an August afternoon and I'd been given permission to play at the Swans while mother was sweeping our front walkways. I'd recently acquired a toy popgun that I wanted the Swan girls to see. Like an old shotgun it hinged in the middle so you could cock the gun and pull the cork-on-a-string into the barrel for another shot. The cork would only fly a few inches—unless you freed it from its tether. This, of course, is just what we did. Then we discovered that a small unattached pebble would fly several feet further than the cork. This new and improved ammunition had many uses. We discovered that it was excellent for blossom blasting. It also made for a great game of shotgun tag. Once, when no adults were looking, Renee guided us on a cat-hunting safari. This game was a short one. It didn't take *Tabby* long to disappear for the day. She returned the next day apparently unscathed by our poor marksmanship.

In the thrill of this new discovery, I began to collect our more effective ammo by bending over the edge of the curb and reaching into the gutter of the street. I knew I was not allowed in the street. I also knew that if I stepped off the curb, my mother's watchful eye would spot me breaking the law. My passport to the Swans' house would be cancelled, and I would be placed under house arrest in my own front yard. This made getting the pebbles difficult. I bent over the curb careful not to actually go into the street. I'm sure Mom didn't realize exactly what we were doing except that I was getting dangerously close to the street.

Mom stopped sweeping to more closely assess the situation just as Cheryl and Renee's father came out of the front door of his house.

"Hello," he said to me.

"Hello, Mr. Swan," I responded.

He then walked around the back side of his old black four-door Packard sedan. Having greeted him, I squatted on the curb hidden behind his front right fender to fetch another pebble. I reached out with my arm in an unsteady position to grab a rock and reload. What happened then, as my mother watched helplessly from three houses away, caught us all by complete surprise.

Mr. Swan entered his car on the street side, looked through the windshield, and saw no children ahead of him (because I was hunched down, reaching out in front of his tire), he started the car. He put his foot on the gas and lumbered away from the curb.

As people stood speechlessly staring in frozen terror, his right front wheel rolled over my chest. He later said that he felt nothing as the front bumper toppled me from the curb into the street in front of the car. He continued on, looking for me in the front yard and feeling only a slight bump as his right rear tire passed over my body.

Mom had viewed the accident helplessly from fifty yards away. Her mother's eyes had seen the car hit me in the side, tumbling me over on my back. She saw that heavy old Packard lumber to a stop with my limp body lying in the street motionless behind the rear bumper. She immediately began to scream, run, and pray at the same time.

The next thing I remember I was in the arms of my mother sitting on her lap. She was in the passenger seat of Mr. Swan's Packard and he was racing to the hospital. I was trying to catch my breath but I couldn't. My lungs seemed to refuse to fill with air.

Mother held me firmly in her arms and kept whispering.

"It's okay, hon, you'll be okay, just breathe. We're going to the hospital."

I remember only two more things that day besides being held in Mom's lap and speeding to the hospital. The first was the warm feel of a wet plaster cast which they put on my right arm in the emergency room. The other was the kind nurse who presented me with my tee-shirt once the tests were over. She smiled and pointed out the tread marks that the tire had left across the chest of my shirt.

A broken arm was the only injury I sustained that day. That old Packard was an exceptionally heavy car, but being so young, my bones and organs were so flexible that I suffered nothing more than a broken arm—and a soiled tee-shirt. I don't even remember being stiff or sore afterward. When the cast came off, I was as good as new.

I have known teens and toddlers, and even newborns whose lives have touched me deeply yet their days on earth were far shorter than mine. They lived and died and I have attended their memorial services and gone on to remember them for years. I believe they, too, were intentional winners in the race of life. They, too, were given the incredible gift of surpassing the odds just to become a person. I believe that for them also, being here wasn't just luck. I believe God knows their names!

Perhaps some of them finished their *course* early because they were better students. Perhaps there is another reason. What I do know is that if I spend too much time wondering *why*, I tend to become a grumpy critic in the *soccer stands* when God gave me life to become a better player on the *pitch*.

I also know that when I am in the game and I cry "Foul"—and God rules, "Play on"—there can be no hesitation on my part!

If I stop playing because I do not like the call, others will be affected. If I leave my position to shake my fist at the *umpire*, I only hurt myself and those who must continue to play without me. I can either pout or play but the game continues and in the end I must remember that my vantage point is limited. God's perspective is unlimited and my game is not over yet!

The important thing I take from my longish life is that being born, and every moment thereafter is an unearned and almost unparalleled gift in this nearly breathless universe. The odds have always been against us, but confidently the Psalmist says, that while our days are numbered, God's precious thoughts for us are as countless as the grains of sand on all the beaches of the world. When you believe this life becomes less frightening, and even death is no longer so scary. With David, I believe that *"When I awake, I am still with thee."*[1]

My very young daughter's face once grew bright with a glowing insight. Megan's eyes widened and gleamed at me with certainty.

"I know, Daddy," she paused and her smile broadened as she completed her thought, "God's gift to us is that he gives us life—and our gift to Him is that we give it back!"

I think she was right.

4

TROUBLE AT THE BALL CUPBOARD

The man said, "Let me go; it's daybreak."

Jacob said, "I'm not letting you go 'til you bless me."

The man said, "What's your name?" - He answered, "Jacob."

The man said, "But no longer. Your name is no longer

Jacob. From now on it's Israel (God-Wrestler); you've wrestled with God and you've come through."

GENESIS 32:26–28 MSG

Alvin Butler was the bully of Abraham Lincoln Elementary School. He was a misfit who came to school in the same brown plaid shirt and dirty jeans every day. Who knows what his home life was like—I suspect it wasn't good.

I was the smallest boy in fifth grade and Alvin never missed an opportunity to bump into me in the hallway. He always pretended it was an accident in case a teacher was looking, but the sneer on his face made it clear that he was trying to pick a fight. After a while I just began to brace myself for the *shoulder shots*. This wasn't easy because he was a head taller than me and outweighed me by several pounds. He had a way of being invisible until he unloaded the pointy part of his shoulder right into the soft spot between my collarbone and my chest; I always ended up with a big bruise. I lived on the *lookout* in the hallways and on the stairs but he still managed to ambush me. Just about the time one bruise would start to fade he'd catch me off guard and add a new one.

I didn't want to tattle on him and I didn't want to back down, but most of all, I didn't want to fight him. It was almost a relief when one day it finally came to a showdown at the ball cupboard.

The ball cupboard stood on the far back corner of the school playground. It was actually a small storage shack with shelves for balls and other equipment. There was room inside for one person behind the Dutch door that served as the service counter. The *Ball Monitor* was a different student each day who made sure all the equipment was checked back in after recess.

On the far side of the ball cupboard was a patch of playground that couldn't be seen from any of the school buildings. That hidden section of the yard was the customary place for after-school scuffles.

It was my day to be *Ball Monitor*. My job was to be sure everyone who signed out equipment signed it back in again at the end of recess. That's how Alvin cornered me. Suddenly, there he was—my worst nightmare—right in front of the line.

Instead of checking his football back in, he was threatening not to give it back. He looked me straight in the eye and said, "Give me the clipboard. I'm writing my name down but I'm not giving you the ball."

I refused to give him the clipboard until I got the ball back on the shelf. He looked over his shoulder at all the kids listening in line behind him. Staring back at me, he said in a loud voice for everyone to hear, "Okay, tough guy, meet me right here behind the ball cupboard after school and we'll settle this."

Word got around quickly.

"Fight behind the ball cupboard after school," the whispers echoed through the hallways.

Alvin had literally forced me into a corner, the corner behind the ball cupboard!

Alvin was not a wrestler; he was a boxer. I'd seen what one kid looked like after he fought with Alvin. Alvin *sucker punched* him first and sent his unsuspecting victim off holding his nose and crying. I still remember the dotted red path on the ground behind him.

The hours after lunch dragged on miserably. There was no escaping the school bell which for me was going to signal *Round One* of a *one-round fight*. All I could think about was my destiny with doom. No matter what the teacher was talking about, my mind was on worst-case survival techniques. Kids kept staring at me with ominous looks as though they were looking at a prized turkey that was about to be plucked, stuffed, and roasted.

I wanted to run. I considered telling a teacher and getting temporary protection but that wouldn't stop Alvin. He'd still be there the next day scoffing at me and bumping me in the halls. Furthermore, not showing up for the fight would tell all the kids that I was *chicken.*

In the end I knew if I avoided him, he'd just be waiting for me another day—but I wouldn't know which day. It was better to suffer the bloody nose and get it over with.

I did consider one alternative strategy. My uncle, Jack, had been a wrestler in high school. The high point of his wrestling career was that he was the only opponent in the state of Pennsylvania who had avoided being pinned by the eventual *state champ.* Uncle Jack's strategy was to run from him the whole match. He didn't even try to win the contest; he just kept trying not to get caught in a hold.

Contrary to boxing folklore, evidently in wrestling *you can't hide but you CAN run*! My uncle was a legendary hero in our family—for not losing too badly!

My hope was to continue that grand family tradition. I wasn't sure this strategy could work for me in a playground fight against a boxer, but it was all I had.

There was one wrestling hold that Uncle Jack taught me. In fact it's the only wrestling hold I ever learned. It was called a "Full Nelson." It's when you are able to get behind your opponent and thrust your arms under his armpits and then lock your fingers behind the base of his neck. Once in place you're pulling his arms back and pushing his head forward at the same time. If you do this successfully, you end up behind your opponent, fitting him like a tortoise shell while his arms wave helplessly in the air. If he tries to get out, you just push forward on his head, forcing his chin into his chest using the pressure against his flailing arms as leverage.

Realistically, I knew Alvin would never let me get behind him to apply a "Full Nelson." After thinking it over, I decided that running and trying not to lose too badly was my best shot!

I'd never been in a fight before. This would be my first, and after the extensive injuries that Alvin would inflict, it would probably be my last. As the school bell rang at the end of the day, I found myself walking through the crowded halls as others sympathetically watched me. I felt like a *dead man walking* across the play yard to the distant ball cupboard.

As I stepped to the back side of the building—the part that was hidden from the school offices—there was a cluster of about ten kids who had formed a circle. There in the middle of the *ring* was Alvin Butler in his soiled plaid shirt which he was about to further soil—with me.

"Let me take off my glasses," I said, walking toward him.

I handed them to a kid standing in the circle and before I could fully turn around, Alvin lunged at me. I knew Alvin would make the first move. I was ready for him. Like my wrestling Uncle Jack before me I was small, but I had one big advantage—I was also slow!

Dodging out of Alvin's path, one leg dragged perilously behind the rest of my body and inexplicably Alvin tripped himself on it. I saw Alvin's face as he went down: it was flushed and angry and a little surprised to be so off balance.

To the crowd this awkward dodge on my part looked like a well-crafted ninja move. In reality, it was nothing but slow reflexes and incredible luck. In that instant as Alvin lay face down in the dirt I knew I had only one option left. I dove on his back before he could get up. Instinctively from wrestling with my Uncle, I slid both my arms under Alvin's armpits from behind and interlocked my fingers at the base of his skull. Miraculously, I had Alvin Butler in a "Full Nelson."

Alvin quickly responded by trying to throw me off. He rolled over on his back hoping to crush me with his weight but I held on for dear life. Like a beetle on his back, Alvin's arms and legs were swimming in the air and I was pinned on my back beneath him. I was like a bull rider holding on for dear life to keep from being thrown and trampled. Alvin was like a flailing snow angel carrying a small human backpack.

He rolled and struggled and began to swear and tell me what he was going to do to me when he got me off his back. This of course scared me to death so I held on tighter. As I did, my locked hands pushed Alvin's chin hard against his chest. Instantly to my surprise, he stopped resisting and went limp. His arms and legs relaxed and he began to cry out, "Okay, okay, stop!"

I loosened my grip just a little, and Alvin wilted into compliance as we both fell motionless—still connected on our sides.

He tried to surprise me a couple times by starting up again but I was too scared not to be ready. Each time he launched a counterattack I'd tighten my grip, Alvin would feel the pressure, and his body would go limp as spaghetti.

I knew that I didn't dare let go. It was either hold on at all cost or die. I had him, but if I let go, he was so mad I knew he would mop the playground with me. I was committed. I was not brave; I was just too scared to let go!

This cycle continued for a long time, each revolt ending in a long motionless rest as we laid in the grass and the dirt. At first the quick *take-down* had been entertaining to the spectators. Alvin was cussing and screaming about what he was going to do to me when he got loose. Now the crowd grew restless as we both lay *stock-still* on the ground; they wanted me to let go and do it again. They expected a little more action; like a bloody nose.

"Come on," someone said, "let him up and fight."

"I am fighting," I said. This was literally true; this was the only fight I had.

After about twenty minutes the kids began to drift away. Nothing was happening. As long as Alvin didn't struggle, all there was to see were two guys lying motionless on the ground.

Now and then Alvin would shriek out in frustration, "Let me up and I'll...."

"No way," I'd say, quietly so no one could hear the fear in my voice.

Alvin struggled—I'd put on more pressure.

He'd stop—we'd both lay there.

Finally the last kid, the one to whom I'd given my glasses, complained.

"I've got to get home. I'm leaving your glasses here on the grass."

"Okay," I said, "See you tomorrow. Thanks."

Alvin muttered something from below but he was spitting grass from his mouth at the same time so it was hard to understand.

The shadows were growing longer. It was getting darker and now all the kids had gone home. We were alone behind the ball cupboard—waiting, I hoped, not until sunrise.

I wondered how long this could go on. I couldn't stay here forever; my mother would already be wondering where I was. I worried that the moment I let go, Alvin would rise up like a wounded lion and leave only my bleached bones behind. I was prepared to stay there until dawn unless he promised me sincerely that the fight was over and we were done for good.

After a long silence I quietly asked him, "Do you give?

I expected him to meet that request with another attempt to break free. I braced myself but surprisingly there was no more fight left in him. He lay there with his limbs dangling—numb from the pressure.

"Okay," he said very quietly. "You win, just let me go."

I thought for a moment—"No, not until you promise this is over…no more fighting, no more bumping in the halls."

"Yeah, yeah, okay, just let me go," he replied, his voice cracking slightly at the end.

That still wasn't enough for me.

"If I let you go and you come at me again…you'll really be sorry," I said.

I was hoping that he was in so much pain that he might actually believe I could do this to him again if necessary. Alvin's voice was softer now. I could see that his fingertips were white from loss of circulation.

"Okay, just let go!" he said.

With the butterflies in my stomach colliding into one another, I began to slowly release my grip. I gave one final warning.

"Remember, you promised, no more fighting—or else!"

My arms came out from under his and I jumped to my feet prepared to see Alvin jump up and come at me fists flailing.

Instead, Alvin groaned as he stood up very carefully. He looked like an old man with arthritis getting out of bed in the morning. He groaned and turned toward me in *slow motion,* rigid and apparently afraid a sudden movement might break something. There was a single tear rolling down each of Alvin's dirty cheeks. I'd never seen Alvin cry before. It was immediately clear that these tears were not the result of humiliation—Alvin was in pain!

I'd let go, but the punishment was continuing! Alvin's arms were frozen in place. I don't know how long he'd been molded in a hands-over-head position, like the victim of an endless stage coach robbery, but Alvin was still *reaching for the sky*. I could tell just from looking at him that his neck hurt, his arms hurt—everything hurt! As he turned to walk home, I watched him try once again to lower his arms. The elbows dipped for an instant and then just as quickly went back into the air again. Alvin resembled a scarecrow that was being transformed into a human except for his stubborn scarecrow arms.

The next day at school I expected Alvin to come after me with a vengeance but that never happened. Instead, something really strange followed. He left me alone. He never bumped me in the hall. He never cursed me or threatened to fight me again. Once, later that year, he even nodded to me as we passed in the hallway; without thinking, I nodded back—it felt good.

Jacob, the old *deceiver,*[1] learned that; sometimes, just holding on until morning is enough for a new start. God changed Jacob's name after their wrestling match. The new name He gave him was Israel. It became the name by which all his descendents are known to this day. Israel means, *"God Wrestler."*[2] It's an odd name for a devout believer, isn't it? Or is it? Amazingly, even though Jacob walked away with a limp, you get the feeling he was better off for the brawl. You sense that what he learned from the scuffle wasn't to overcome his fear of the darkness but rather just to tighten his grip in the midst of it, even if it was only because he was too scared to let go. Sometimes faith is little more than holding on until dawn!

Every believer bumps into their own personal *Alvin Butler*; this world is filled with all kinds of them. When the time comes to face them, we strangely discover that we are stronger than we thought—God is closer than we imagined—and in this life, there is often no blessing without wrestling.

5

HOME BEFORE DARK

The Spirit of God, who raised Jesus from the dead, lives in you...

And I am convinced that nothing can ever separate us from God's love.

Neither death nor life, neither angels nor demons, neither our fears for today nor our worries about tomorrow—not even the powers of hell can separate us from God's love.

No power in the sky above or in the earth below—indeed,
nothing in all creation will ever be able to separate us from
the love of God that is revealed in Christ Jesus our Lord.

ROMANS 8:11, 38–39 NLT

I don't know when my fear of the darkness began. I just remember that as a child, there was always a night light in my room to keep me safe.

Summer twilights always seemed safe as I ran through fields with friends in the lingering alpenglow of sunset. The aroma of tall grass, evening barbeques, and hand-cranked strawberry ice cream charmed those endless evenings. Fall sunsets brought a different childhood memory. Brilliant backlit trees with amber leaves gave way to lengthening shadows. As night fell, those same brilliant trees became dark rangy-armed monsters lining the streets waiting for children who had foolishly played too long at school.

Autumn hints at Halloween. Centuries ago as darkness fell at this time of year, people would remember those who had once lived with vitality who were now only a shadowy memory. In dread they celebrated the missing with the *Day of the Dead*. Christian believers preferred the more hopeful title, *All Saints Day*.

Getting home before dark was a rule that I was always happy to follow! I preferred the warm light of home to the sudden eclipse of autumn evenings.

My return to school each fall was accompanied by a recurring nightmare. In the dream I would stay too late on the playground and on the walk home, the sun would begin to set and the darkness would begin to close in around me. I would try to walk faster but my legs dragged behind me as though they were *postholing* through a snowfield. The night would slowly overtake me before I could get home. When I finally reached the front door it felt like midnight, all the lights were out and darkness reigned. I always got there, but the dream always ended with my hand on the shadowy doorknob. I never remember opening the door to safety and a well-lit welcome. That is, I never remember opening the door until one scary October night that stands out above all the others.

It began like most other Sunday evenings. It was youth group night at church, and I walked the three short blocks from my home in the late afternoon. The junior high group met in a large house on the corner of the church lot. We would gather in the spacious living room and play games and sing songs. Just before the snacks were served, one of the youth leaders would read from the Bible and explain how they related to the passage. Looking back now, I don't remember many of those talks. What I do remember are the Bible verses that were planted in me like magic beans buried in a field. Those seedlings still sprout into my memory today; they were not annuals—they are perennials.

Sometimes the leaders were young, like Cal Varner who was still in college. Sometimes the leaders were older like Mr. Gunn who must have been in his seventies at the time. We called him by his preferred nickname—*Pop Gunn*. These leaders, for some inconceivable reason, loved rowdy junior high kids like me and they saturated us with love and the Bible.

As the days grew shorter, approaching the winter solstice, the leaders would drive us home after the youth meeting. On this particular night, the house was jammed with kids and that meant that their cars would also be jammed with kids needing rides home. Since I lived so close to the church, I bravely volunteered to walk home. After all I was thirteen, it was only three blocks, and it wasn't dark yet—I thought! As I opened the front door to begin my journey, the darkness slapped me in the face. It was later than I realized.

While the Youth House sat on the corner of well-lit Garey Avenue, I had to make a quick left and follow Pasadena Street which was more dimly lit and far less populated. It was at the end of Pasadena Street that the real challenge came. A right turn put me onto Main Street.

The problem was Main Street was not a *main* street. No doubt somewhere in my small town Main Street was busier and well-lit, but here in the residential north side of town it was anything but *main*. It was more like *Minor Street*. Main was so *minor* that only one solitary lamppost on the east side lit the sidewalk for the entire block. The streetlamp on the west side of the street had burned out.

I stopped and huddled safely at the base of the lamplight for a moment. All the houses across the street from me were embedded in ghostly darkness. Trees that brought welcome shade to the street in the daytime now slowly moved in the night breeze, casting ominous shadows from the streetlamp in every direction. I stood nervously under the spotlight and watched the path before me disappear into the murky shadows in the distance.

I remember what happened next with crystal clarity. Standing in the light of the lamppost, I looked into the darkness and nervously thought, *The worst thing that can happen if I walk over to the dark side of the street is that I could die in the shadows, BUT if I do die, I'll still be with God! Dead or alive, I belong to Him!*

I remember this unusual thought from so many years ago because it surprised me. It was after nightfall and I was afraid of the dark! The only reason this risky thought came to me at all was that the seeds planted in my brain in youth group that night seemed to have found fertile soil: *"Nothing in all creation will ever be able to separate us from the love of God...."*[1]

On the surface it made every bit of sense to stay on the best-lit, *safe* side of the street for my journey. This is why I want to warn boys and girls not to do what I did next—*unless* you also encounter a time when God seems to be trying to sprout something deep and new in you.

Before I knew it, my feet had stepped off the curb and I was crossing over to the dark side of the street, the far side—the side where the streetlamp had gone out!

There were no lit porch lights on that side of the street. A single living room window flickered with the dim lone light of a television screen. The oscillating gray beams of the black-and-white TV did not shine through the window and illuminate the street. Instead, like a *black hole*, its shadows seemed to drain the light from around me, drawing it back into the window—leaving me even more isolated in the deep, cool darkness.

My first steps had been slow due to fear; now they quickened with the desire to reach my own front porch as fast as possible. Then, the unexplainable happened: something in me told me to slow my pace to rest in the confidence of the *Holy Darkness* that surrounded me. I began to smile nervously at the absurdity of this whole situation. I scanned the black hedges that neatly bordered the duplexes to my right. How silly of me to be doing the exact opposite of what my head would normally be telling me to do. I should have been sprinting home at full speed like a running back. Instead, I obeyed the quiet direction that was leading me from inside. I intentionally slowed my pace to that of an afternoon stroll. Now, gradually and deliberately, I moved more deeply into the shadows with each step.

The cool night breeze blew, the trees swayed, the lamppost on the far side of the street now grew fainter in the distance behind me. This was a *test*. This was a game with high stakes. This was a contest of conviction. I felt I was no longer walking alone. I heard a voice, not the audible kind, challenge me from within, *trust God or fear the darkness—one or the other—CHOOSE!*

A sudden movement from under one of the hedges rekindled the fear and set my heart pounding. A silhouette bolted from one hedge to another. I stopped and peered into black space. My mind ran wild. *Was it an animal—a raccoon or a badger? Whatever it was, was it just hunting in the night, or was it running from something bigger and more terrifying—something actually stalking ME?*

I chuckled in relief at my imagination as Ginger, my neighbor's cat, padded up to me in the darkness and rubbed her raised back on my leg. *Oh, good,* I thought, *it's just you and me, Ginger—you and me and the darkness.* The darkness lingered—Ginger did not!

My last turn was a left onto Pearl Street. I stepped off the dark curb to cross the street and conquer the final blackened block. The trees that lined each side of the street locked their boney fingers, forming a canopy over my head. An autumn breeze moaned through the arching tree-tunnel—then, just as suddenly, the wind became breathless.

I froze in the middle of the deserted road quiet as a ghost. I turned and peered backward for my last look at the single, distant street-light—the left turn ahead of me would cause the friendly glow to vanish behind the gray houses that lined the block.

Slow now, and no shortcuts, the silent voice within me whispered. I straightened my angle and did not cut the corner to save time. I forced myself to walk straight across the street. Stepping onto the sidewalk I squared my shoulders, executed a *left face,* and turned toward home.

One more step and I was MORE than halfway—I took it—the die was cast. Now there was as much distance behind me to the vanished lamppost as there was before me to my house. The path ahead was the last and darkest leg of my journey.

No turning back! Again, the quiet voice reassured me.

No need to hurry—breathe—one step at a time.

My house was on the right side, second in from the far corner, nearly a full *lightless* block away—but the fear had lessened. I could see more detail in the dark than when my eyes were constantly darting back to the shining security of the light. I could now see stars twinkling above the clearings in the tree branches. It seemed brighter to me at night than I had ever realized before. The pale moon was bathing the surfaces of the neighborhood with the reflected light of the sun. The houses looked familiar in the softened glow. I began to hum a tune in my head. It was one of the choruses I had learned in youth group. I wasn't just *whistling a happy tune* in the dark. I was singing to *Someone—Someone* whose helpful haunting was lighting my way home.

I turned at our walkway and climbed the stairs to our front porch. I faced the long-awaited door and put my hand on the knob—then wistfully—I pulled back. I turned toward the street one more time and put my hands in my pockets. I stood quietly in the silence. My eyes surveyed the trees, the leaves, the long deserted street, and the path I had traveled. Artificial lights were no longer visible—I had turned more than one corner.

Moonlight, starlight, and the inaudible Spirit had led the way home. I stood for what seemed a long time staring out from under the porch overhang. Finally I took a calm, deep breath and turned the doorknob. I knew the house would be flooded with light and the smell of Mom's homemade chili. I opened the door and went in.

That walk in the dark was sixty years ago, but it changed my life in three important ways:

First, I no longer use a bedside light to help me feel safe. I sleep better in the dark now. To me, the darkness seems close and comforting like a blanket, like a warm partner who huddles closer as the light fades.

Second, I never again had that scary dream about rushing home from school after sunset and being overcome by the shadows—not even once!

Finally, that walk taught me that this journey we are on is never completely safe and is sometimes frightening; that's why it's best that we travel with a *Silent Partner*. We begin in uncertainty and fear; He whispers counsel and gives courage along the way. In the dark, faith grows by walking—and walking isn't so scary—once you know you are already *home before dark!*

6

DONNIE MCCOY

The eye cannot say to the hand,

   "I have no need of you," nor again the head to the feet,
"I have no need of you."

   On the contrary, the members of the body that seem to
be weaker are indispensible….

I Corinthians 12:21–22

It's been over fifty years, but I will never forget Donnie McCoy. Donnie and I were on a basketball team in high school together. Donnie was the shortest member on the team, but what he lacked in height he made up for in *clumsy*. It's not that Donnie was slow; in fact, he was pretty quick. It's just that he lacked control. We were much more relaxed when Larry Cutler, our star rebounder, or Tim Akers, our jump shot artist, had the ball. When Donnie had the ball, you could never tell what might happen. He'd bounce the ball off his foot, drive to the basket in a fury, then pass the ball to you as hard as he could from three feet away. Both teams had to be ready when Donnie got on the court. Donnie dribbled to a different drummer!

Still, we all loved Donnie because whatever else he lacked, he did not lack confidence! He was so unselfconscious and so resilient that nothing got in the way of his enthusiasm. Donnie gave 100 percent every time he stepped on the court. Nothing was done without intensity; Donnie was ALL heart.

Donnie was a *second stringer*, but he never put himself down and he gave his best every time he was called on. More than once we were behind in a difficult game and Donnie would cheer us on from the bench and we'd think, *If Donnie McCoy can believe this much in us, how can we not believe in ourselves!* With Donnie's voice booming encouragement from the bench, we came from behind many times to clinch a close game and score the victory.

Donnie's positive energy was a fuel additive to our team engine. His attitude made us perform better. We loved Donnie. We loved him more on the bench cheering than on the court playing, but we loved him. Donnie made a difference!

My senior year was especially exciting because we not only qualified for the state playoffs (in our humble church league competition), but thanks to Larry's rebounding and Tim's jump shot, we made our way all the way to the state championship game.

Our opponents had drafted varsity high school ball players after their school season had ended and padded their ranks with these "pros." They had some stars but we played as a team and in the final two minutes of the championship game, the unimaginable had happened—we led by six points.

It wasn't all good news, however. After clearing the backboards for us all night, Larry Cutler fouled out. Now our defense was mortally wounded!

Still there was hope. All we had to do was control the ball and give up no more than five points until the buzzer went off and the championship was ours.

Hal Varner, our coach, surveyed the bench. We needed a replacement for Larry on the court. As Hal's eyes peered down the line of available players, they stopped on the single player left on the bench. Our voices were supportive but our hearts shuddered as he called Donnie's number.

If ball control was the name of the game, Donnie was the wrong player—but our fouls had been plentiful and our ranks were exhausted. Donnie was the only choice left.

Enthusiastically, Donnie jumped to his feet. Nervously, our team began to whisper, "Don't pass to Donnie!"

Once he was on the court, it didn't take long for the other team to find our weakest link. We tried not to pass the ball to Donnie but on a couple of occasions there was no one else open. As the clock ticked, each time Donnie touched the ball he turned it over to the other team. Twice they stole the ball from him and drove the length of the court for easy layups. Our lead dropped to four points and then to two—then, without Larry's rebounding, the game was tied.

They just kept at Donnie, but he never showed any sign of frustration; he just kept giving us the best that he had. It didn't seem to faze him that he'd turned the ball over enough times to tie the game. He didn't get sullen and defeated. He just kept playing with all his heart. Donnie was doing what Donnie always did. He was going *all out*— Donnie was not a quitter!

With the score even and seconds left to play, something amazing happened. The other team inbounded the ball for what was to be their final play. Their ball handler having seen Donnie's lack of control underestimated his frenetic quickness. In a last-ditch effort, Donnie stuck his hand out—and stole the ball!

With only ten seconds on the clock, the players on the bench were screaming. All of us on the court were waving our hands and staring wide-eyed at Donnie. Donnie looked stunned, not sure himself about what had just happened. Everyone in the building was standing!

Immediately, the other team was on Donnie but he resisted dribbling. Soon he was double-teamed, but he just kept pivoting to keep the ball from his opponents.

The clock ticked down to seven seconds. He looked to pass the ball but everyone was covered.

It was a tie game with most of our best players out—and Donnie McCoy holding the ball at half court. We all knew that if this game went into overtime, we were *goners*.

The last six seconds were an eternity. Everyone was yelling and screaming. In desperation Coach Varner shouted from the sidelines, "Shoot it, Donnie; shoot it!"

Considering the fact that no one had ever heard our coach yell these instructions to Donnie before, his response was astounding. Donnie obeyed so quickly that his opponents barely saw him leave the ground. He sprang abruptly into the air, turning himself toward the basket as he rose from the half-court line. The globe exploded out of his hands like a cannonball—five seconds, four seconds.

As the clock ticked down to three seconds, the ball came down six feet short and seven feet wide of the basket. Donnie had, of course, been aiming for the rim—instead, like a *Hail Mary Pass*, the ball landed perfectly in the hands of Tim Akers, whose jump shot passed through the net just at the sound of the buzzer—*bull's-eye*! Nothing but net! Game! Win! STATE CHAMPIONSHIP!

I don't remember who was awarded the game ball that night, but there is no doubt that Donnie McCoy was the *most valuable player* on that team for teaching me an essential truth about life. Donnie never tried to be Larry Cutler or Tim Akers, but he was the best Donnie McCoy that team could have ever had!

A *second stringer* in the Houston Symphony once told me, "No one likes to be called *Second Fiddle*." (Second violinists play the lower string harmonies to the first violinist's lilting melodies.)

"But," she continued, "I tell my students what my teacher taught me, 'Sit in the seat that's open to you and lead from the chair you're sitting in.'"

Donnie did just that. The chair he led from was usually the team bench—but bench or court, he gave *Coach* the best he had. When we do that, the Bible says, *It's nothing but net!*

7

GHOST HIKE

Rejoice with me, for I have found my sheep that was lost.

LUKE 15:6B

In the late 1960s, I worked at a summer camp that hosted almost two thousand elementary schoolchildren every season. When I think about all those kids and that immense mountain wilderness, I'm amazed at the fact that we never lost one of them! I know that it would be unacceptable for a camp director to lose even one camper. Still, I marvel at the fact that every Sunday afternoon at least one hundred kids would roll into camp and the next Saturday morning every single one of them returned home (the same child to the same home)! There was, however, one very close call.

One year we reserved the final week of summer camp for a large number of kids who lived in a nearby inner city where people were poor and life could be dangerous. These children may have been economically disadvantaged but they were alert, attentive, and emotionally transparent. The majesty of the mountains that surrounded them filled them with wonder. When they spotted a cumulus cloud, a stream, or a squirrel, they reacted like Christopher Columbus at the sight of land. They were in awe of EVERYTHING, and they seldom had a thought that they didn't feel compelled to express.

On the other hand, at times they were as cautious in the mountains as I would have been on the streets of Chicago's South Side. Often they had more *savvy* than the affluent kids who had filled most of our camps that summer. These city kids lived by a self-preservation instinct in their neighborhoods; they knew how to protect themselves when they sensed danger. They knew when to *come* and they knew when to *run*!

All this made for a great mutual learning experience. They lived in teepees for the week and learned about Native Americans; I learned to rediscover the transparent beauty of honest expression and genuine affection.

This mix of inner-city culture and mountain summer camp meant their week was different from the other camps that summer. When Moses Poolaw, our ancient Kiowa Indian, gave his testimony in camp about his misspent years of living as a bar brawler and a professional baseball player, these kids were not as spellbound as the kids from the suburbs.

Mose had been born in a teepee and had no knowledge of how old he was but judging from the lines in his face, he rivaled Methuselah. He stood before the camp in authentic Indian costume (with the exception of barely visible boxer shorts with tiny red firemen peeking out from under his leather leggings.) Usually when Mose lifted his shirt and showed the bullet holes from his life of riotous living, our *uptown* campers would look on in astonishment. Not these city kids; they'd seen bullet holes before!

Sometimes these kids brought a whole new vocabulary to camp life. One delightful little girl named Raylene called mosquito bites "itchy bumps." Her descriptive name caught on. We inaugurated an "itchy bump contest" in her honor. She won, of course.

I will never forget her melodic cadence as she counted her way to victory over the competition.

"One hundred seventeen itchy bumps... ONE HUNDRED AND EIGHTEEN ITCHY BUMPS... ONE HUNDRED—AND NINETEEN ITCHY BUMPS!"

The term "mosquito bite" has since that day seemed pathetically inadequate to me.

Another difference was that no food, not even green vegetables, went back to the main kitchen uneaten during this week at camp. All the plates were clean, every morsel, every meal! Many of these kids did not get enough to eat at home, so here at camp nothing escaped them!

The pool and lake had to be guarded very carefully because these kids did not have the privilege of swimming lessons at their family's fancy fitness club. They thrashed at the water trying to stay afloat as *swim time* largely became *learn-to-swim time*.

This week of camp, more than the others, was filled with emotion, joy, and wonder. These were the kind of children Jesus was talking about when he urged adults to become more like kids. These young-sters were thankful, eager, and awed by everything—even "itchy bumps."

On Wednesday evening each week, we followed the evening "Council Fire" with a night hike to the creek and a ghost story. Back then (fifty-plus years ago) I reasoned—*what camp experience would be complete without a late-night ghost story told around a crackling fire?* I thought that the blended emotions of fear and fun, climaxed by the glow of s'mores above the blazing coals, were a *great* ending to a day of adventure.

This particular night hike, like so many other things this week, was to be different! Normally every child brought a flashlight which was on the packing list for camp. Most of these kids did not own a flashlight! Consequently, in the dark, the trail down to the creek was hard to see and the kids were huddled together around their counsel-or's flashlights. We didn't have to wait for the spooky story for some of these already cautious campers to begin to see ghosts!

We made our way to a familiar clearing by the creek side that was surrounded by trees. During the day, the clearing revealed a sunbathed stream bordered by tall alder trees, their soft leaves glimmering in the light. At night these rangy giants loomed above us like ogres of the forest.

We sat the children on the ground and asked everyone to turn out their flashlights. As chief of the Indian Village, I lit the fire in the cen-ter of the huddled tribe and began to tell the ghost story. The campfire projected our twisted shadows onto the white-barked monsters that encircled us. I left my single flashlight on, holding it eerily under my chin to cast a grotesque shadow on my face as I set the stage for the evening's high point.

Exposed in the flickering light, the campers clung to their counselors like sheep crowding their shepherd at the approach of a mountain lion. Without a single city light to penetrate the darkness, there was an uneasiness overtaking the clan. I should have noticed the abnormal discomfort in the tribe. This was not the usual air of nervous anticipation about the ghost story to come!

I told the story just as I had told it to the previous nine camps that summer.

"Once, long ago on this mountain there were Indians who traded fur pelts from their winter's hunting to a merchant from the trading post in the valley. The trader would journey into the mountain canyon once each year to barter for the beautiful leather and warm fur. Often he would deceive the Indians, cheating them out of a fair trade for the colored beads and steel tools which the maidens and the braves desired. One day the chief's son grew angry and tired of the fur trader's dishonesty. He waited for the cover of nightfall and then snuck up on the trader from behind in this very clearing where we sit. He grabbed the fur trader with one hand and drew his knife with the other. The fur trader was quick and strong; he struggled with the young brave. The attacker was only able to take a patch of hair from his scalp before the trader escaped his grasp. But it was too late; the attack had driven the fur trader forever mad. He ran into this forest moaning from his wound—and though it has been many long moons, it is said that he still wanders this creek bed tormented and in search of his enemy. From time-to-time people report that they have seen and heard him in the forest-darkness gazing at the stars and howling at the moon."

It was in this part of the story that, twenty-five yards off in the dark, Swift Eagle—one of our staff counselors—began to moan in a low torturous tone. His haunting voice grew more intense as he came closer and the story reached its climax.

At this point in the *tall tale*, all the children in the preceding camps that summer had nervously huddled closer to their counselors for protection. Then, just as they were about to scream, Swift Eagle would step into the fire light right behind me. Recognizing him with a huge sigh of relief, everyone would see the joke, have a good laugh, and join in *s'mores* and singing around the campfire.

Like many other things this particular week, these kids reacted differently. When I got to the part of the story where Swift Eagle began to moan in the distance, these kids were not *nervous*—they were *TERRIFIED*! At Swift Eagle's first moan, the entire camp froze motionless and a hundred pair of white saucerlike eyes peered through me, trying to penetrate the darkness behind me. At the onset of his second agonizing groan one of the kids, no doubt one who had encountered disturbed people before, stood to his feet and shouted, "IT'S HIM! RUN!"

Instantaneously, one hundred campers let go of their counselors and bolted in the opposite direction into the dark woods behind them. The entire tribe was running over rocks, climbing over boulders and dashing though groves of stinging nettle plants. All we heard was the thunder of footsteps in the sand, the sound of breaking branches, and a stampede of sneakers splashing through the stream. The pandemonium was followed by ominous silence as their feet outdistanced our ears.

The counselors and I stood there stunned in the quiet glow of the deserted campfire. Swift Eagle bounced out from the bushes behind me, but there were no children left to see him. There was no sense of relief, no laughter. S'mores and camp songs were the furthest thing from our minds.

Swift Eagle looked at us, we looked at him—spontaneously we began to yell.

"Come back, it's a joke—it's a make-believe story." No one was near enough to hear us!

We left the campfire and began to fan out in every direction except the one from which Swift Eagle had come. We kept yelling into the echoing wilderness.

Thankfully, after a few tense minutes, one and two at a time, the kids began to trickle back to the campfire. We tried to comfort and assure them that this was all in *fun* but this was an uphill battle! Swift Eagle had to impersonate the groaning of the fur trader before some of them reluctantly began to believe it was his voice they had heard. The camp nurse treated abrasions and nettle stings. Over the next fifteen minutes the counselors, who had now gone deep into the forest, returned, bringing the majority of the not-so-brave—*braves* and *maidens* back to the campfire. Each time one was returned, we recounted the whole group just to be certain.

Finally, ninety-nine campers were safely in the fold. Only one was still lost in the darkness and we quickly realized who was absent—it was Raylene, our energetic "itchy-bump girl." Our lost sheep had a name.

No one even thought to suggest that ninety-nine campers were enough. Knowing now who was missing only intensified the search. I sent all the counselors into the darkness to continue the search while I led the gathered campers in a chant. Echoing from the streambed, under the stars and over the rocks, the collective call went out in one rhythmic voice.

"Raylene, come back—Raylene, come back—Raylene, come back!"

It was several tense minutes before our precious stray who had run for her life and then climbed a tree made her way back. In a moment filled with anxious suspense, the waiting crowd saw the shrubs that encircled the campfire move; Raylene emerged stepping into the fire-lit clearing. The worried crowd erupted with shrieks of joy. She was hugged and kissed and patted on the back. The "itchy-bump girl" had been found. Once again, we would return one camper for every one who'd come to camp!

That was the last ghost hike of the summer; it also turned out to be the last ghost hike ever at Indian Village...*period*! I worked at Forest Home many more summers, and our inner-city kids returned each year but we decided that this was not an experience we wanted to repeat. It was too scary for the children, but it was just as frightening to me.

I thought to myself—*What if someone had been seriously hurt or became lost beyond finding*? All these children were in my charge, not most but all were in my care. Had I lost only one child in all those summers, that would be the child I would have remembered forever!

I have come to realize that in the times when I have felt distant from God, when I have been lost and isolated in some self-made wilderness, I am not the only one who feels the distance. If I hate to lose things, God must all the more suffer when the people he loves are not where they should be. The most frightening story to him is that we might choose to stay forever huddled in the darkness having run until we can run no more, separated from Him and overwhelmed by fear. If I, a lad in my twenties with less than perfect judgment, could not leave Raylene behind without feeling devastating loss, how much more is God motivated to call our name when we have wandered off?

If you have ever been scared and alone in the dark, you know it is no joke. If you have ever been lost or if you are lost right now, if you feel abandoned, bruised, and isolated, you know it is not funny; it is frightening. But if you listen, you will hear a voice ringing out over boulders and streams, through forests of nettles and under every star. He knows YOU by name and He is calling you home. You can hear His call deep inside no matter how far away you have run. If you are distant today it is YOU, not the found ones, who occupy His heart the most. All the others are not enough for Him; he waits for your embrace. Your search PARTY is ready to begin with joyous laughter and lavish celebration. God does not *round up* and call it *close enough* at ninety-nine!

This is the story Jesus told about the lost sheep. This is the story Mose Poolaw told about his life. This is my story—and it's your story too! He never gives up until the last lost Indian is found. He loves us this much, "itchy bumps" and all.

8

FIRE ON THE HILL

You are the light of the world ... let your light shine before others, so that they may see your good works and give glory to your Father in heaven.

MATTHEW 5:13–16

I've had a lot of different jobs in my life, including life guard, Indian chief, and harbor master! I haven't been a *beacon of light* in everything I have done—but God has taught me that even if we just show up, *He can shine a little light wherever we go.*

After graduating from seminary, I was called to a church in Vancouver, British Columbia, to work with kids. The best part of the job was that for three months every summer I was to be our denomination's camp director at a humble little summer camp set high on a hill.

I was minimally qualified to do this because while in seminary, I'd spent my summers running a boys' camping program in the mountains of Southern California. The California camp was organized around an American Plains Indian theme. We lived in canvas teepees and divided up to two hundred campers each week into six tribes. They were led by *tribal chiefs* (staff counselors), who in turn were each responsible for four *clan chiefs* (local church counselors), who looked after six young *braves* each.

I was *Chief Black Knife*. I carried a big, black-handled Bowie knife sheathed in a white rabbit pelt. I had sun-bleached blond hair and, except for *photo ops*, I wore dark-rimmed glasses. I may not have looked like an Indian to adults but to fifth grade boys, the Bowie knife made me as genuine as Geronimo!

The camp I was now to direct in British Columbia was on a scenic island, a short ferryboat hop from the mainland. It was lush with plants and trees, hardly the habitat for Plains Indians.

Undaunted, I had the youthful confidence of a twenty-five-year old seminary graduate and a zeal for Christian camping. Along with many dedicated leaders, we began an uphill run to bring necessary improvements to the stagnant camping program and its rickety old buildings. I took everything I knew from Forest Home's Indian Village and plagiarized it (with their blessing) for Keats Island Camp.

The theme was not Plains Indians but *high-sea adventure*. The guest speakers were not *chiefs* but *admirals*. The lead counselors were not *clan chiefs* but *ship captains*. The church counselors were not *tribal chiefs* but *skippers*, and the campers were not *braves* but *mates*.

Instead of *Chief Black Knife* complete with feathered headdress, I was now *Harbor Master Ed*, with a gold-braided cap and brass-buttoned blue blazer.

There was some opposition to me as a newcomer from *south of the border* bringing so much change to the rustic old Canadian camp. In the end, the progressive board backed me on all the changes I proposed and added some of their own. One influential board member was so excited that he got his whole family to commit to financing a complete facelift of the camp.

The cabins were remodeled and moved to create communities, which we called *fleets*. Here the kids could gather in small living clusters and build relationships through the morning activities.

The *Ship's Galley* was expanded for dining and a new meeting room and bell tower were connected by a raised boardwalk that lined the crest of the hill and linked all the main buildings together. A fresh coat of nautical blue covered all the old paint-peeled buildings! By the second summer, the camp that had struggled to find enough campers to operate was now sold out in advance every week. Having shamelessly stolen all I knew from the Indian Village at Forest Home, I was hailed as an imaginative genius. (I graciously accepted the praise!)

The first summer staff was small and they worked from *reveille* to *taps*. In the mornings they led hikes and told Bible stories. In the evenings, they led skits and songs and gave devotional talks by the campfire. In the afternoons, they were the lifeguards for the waterfront play.

When the time came for training them in their lifesaving

certification, I gathered them at the waterfront. I had earned my life-guard instruction certification in the warm waters of a California pool. As I taught these students from an open ocean wharf, I failed to notice how blue they were turning in the icy waters of British Columbia. One of them came near to a serious renal failure because of his dedication to succeed and his unwillingness to complain. In spite of my nearly killing him off, Rob Bentall founded a second conference center thirty years ago. He has given his life to the Lord in ministry to couples and families.

Rob and I are blood brothers, bearing scars from our maintenance duties without a doctor close enough to provide stitches. Butterfly bandages were all we had time for, so the short scar on his nose and the long one on my shin still show.

I acquired a less visible wound the day I decided to promote our waterfront competition with an Olympics skit. It was the summer of '72 and the Olympic Games were in Germany, but everyone knew they were coming to Canada in '76! It seemed timely to use the energy of the Olympics to bring excitement to our activities that afternoon down at the wharf.

I primed the staff to ring the bell before lunch and gather the camp in the chow line in front of the *Ship's Galley*. They were to direct the campers' attention to the Olympic runner (me), who was to streak his way up the steep hill to herald the afternoon waterfront games.

I put on running shorts, tennis shoes, and a tank top shirt to look like a sprinter. For a torch I soaked a rag in gasoline and tied it to the end of a sawed off broom stick. It was now late summer and the grass was a little dry on the hill leading up to the dining hall. As the bell pealed at the top of the hill and the children watched intently, I lit the torch and began my run from the docks below.

It was a brilliant summer day, so it was hard to see the fire at the top of the torch but the kids got the idea and began to cheer me on. The hill was straight up and I soon realized that my first mistake was that I had failed to train for a 150-yard uphill sprint with a flaming torch. My stamina began to weaken after the first twenty-five steep steps, but the kids were clapping and screaming—the show had to go on!

I was giving it my all and feeling pretty warmed up when I noticed that my torch-holding hand felt warmer than the rest of me. As I approached the halfway mark, I took a closer look and saw why my hand was feeling so hot—it was on fire! The gasoline from the rag at the top of my torch had begun to roll down the broom handle and the fire was following it all the way and licking at my fingers.

The kids were cheering me on enthusiastically! They couldn't see the lapping flames in the brightness of the day; they only saw an Olympic runner (a very slow one) on his way to proclaim an important announcement. I wished that instead of announcing the waterfront event, I had been right in the middle of the waterfront because at that moment there was no water anywhere on that brown grassy uphill stretch.

I had three choices: (1) drop the torch on the dry grass—the island had no fire department; (2) keep switching hands; or (3) tilt the torch backward, run faster, and hope for a headwind to drive the flames back up the stem of the torch. I decided on a combination of switching hands and running faster. By now I was totally exhausted from the incline, but the thought of igniting into full-blown flames gave me new motivation to run. I didn't dare wipe the gas from my hands on to my clothing; I could have instantly become a human lighthouse.

I knew it was time to alternate my hands when I could see a new patch of hair on the back of my arm begin to singe and curl from the flames. I actually didn't have to watch it; I could smell the pungent odor as the tiny hairs curled like papier-mâché in a bonfire. With every whiff my pace quickened. With each stride I began to blow at my torch-holding hand to fan the flame back up the torch. Although I now had twice the oxygen deficit, the safest choice was to keep juggling, blowing, and running. As the finish line came into view and the fire kissed at my fingers, my pace actually quickened to a strong finish. If there was an Olympic event called the *Docks to Dining Hall Dash*, I would have *medaled*!

Just before total combustion, I reached the top of the hill to a massive cheer from the crowd. More importantly, I reached the bucket of water we had positioned earlier to douse the torch.

Having broken the tape, I was so winded that I couldn't speak. The staff stepped in with barely controlled laughter and made the announcement while I soaked my hands in the bucket with the torch. All the hair on my arms was gone; I smelled like gasoline, and I could barely stand upright from exhaustion. It was a scene that would have caused the ancient Greeks to drop their grape clusters and mumble into their wine goblets.

Little did I know that day that some of the flames had licked the dry grass on the way up the hill and were it not for the watchful eye of our maintenance man, who hurried over to dowse them, the entire camp and perhaps all the cottages on the island, in fact the whole island, could have gone up in an Olympic blaze!

In the end, my stupidity was kept under wraps. The games were a success, and even the hair on my arms grew back.

Today, two separate Christian conference centers operate on Keats Island, not just in the summer anymore but year-round. One of them is dedicated primarily to kids; the other is devoted to couples and families. It seems the seeds for one's renewal and the other's birth came from those strategic summers and the labors of all those dedicated people who added their energy to the vision I "stole" from Forest Home. Hundreds of people have heard the good news about Jesus and made decisions to follow Him at those two island retreat centers.

Twenty years later, I was invited back for an anniversary celebration at *Barnabas Landing* and *Keats Island Camp*. I was honored as having made a contribution to their ministries. The folks did not mention that I could have killed off my first staff with my ice-water lifesaving sessions. There was no remembrance that I could have easily burned down the entire island. There was only gratitude, appreciation, and even a little applause. I much preferred this to being run out of Canada as a public nuisance—or serving jail time for arson, reckless endangerment, or worse!

Sometimes, even on our brightest days we lack brilliance. This doesn't seem to be a problem for God. Jesus didn't tell his followers that they *could* be the light of the world or that they *sometimes* were the light of the world—he told them, *"You [ARE] the light of the world."*[1]

We make do the best we can with our faulty torches and try to *stay the course*. He provides the enduring flame and by His grace He guides even our missteps. In the long run, people are drawn to the light that burns brightest.

9

LASER TAG

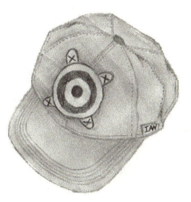

If we say that we have no sin, we deceive ourselves, and the truth is not in us.

If we confess our sins, he who is faithful and just will forgive us our sins and cleanse us from all unrighteousness.

I JOHN 1:8–9

I couldn't remember Freda Fay ever speaking to me directly. Of course, I never spoke to her either. Our family only knew her name because other neighbors had told it to us. Our family was young and we were in our backyard often playing ping-pong and croquet, and throwing catch with any kind of ball that we could find. We would see a shadowy figure working in the garden between the green slats of the backyard fence. Her vegetables were tall and leafy. Freda Fay was *The Phantom of the Okra.* We didn't dislike her; we just never had an occasion to talk to her.

The breakthrough came with the discovery of a great new game. It was called *Laser Tag.* It consisted of several space-age-looking laser guns that projected their red beams at least 30 yards when you pulled the trigger. Each gun came with a separate circular sensor that flashed a very small red light to help you find the target in the dark. I had the brilliant idea of discarding the vests that came with the sensor and sewing them onto baseball caps instead. This way no one could cheat by blocking their targets with their hands or clothing.

The game was simple. My kids and their friends, some of whom brought their own equipment, would divide into two equal teams. Both teams had lasers; both wore the sensor ball caps. The "hunters" counted to one hundred in the front yard, while the "hunted" scurried to find places to hide in our backyard. Then, as the hunters made their way to the back of the house, everyone would try to blast the opposing team's blinking sensors. If your laser beam hit their sensor, it beeped loudly three times; after three hits, the sensor would permanently light up and play an electronic jingle that meant *the party was over* for you until the next round!

Today, some might think this game to be wrong on many levels! I'm told lasers aren't good for your eyes, there are probably better games to teach children, and in today's culture doing something like this in your backyard would be like sending a personal invitation to your local police SWAT team to come join *the hunt.* But this was many decades ago, and it was really fun!

This game became the place to be in our neighborhood. My son's and daughter's friends would come over often after dark to play. All the kids loved it. It was never boring.

Our yard was perfect for the game with lots of trees and objects to hide behind and shield your sensor. There was nothing to squabble about because the electronics told you when you'd been tagged and when you were out of the game.

My favorite hiding spot was in the branches of a leafy towering fig tree. It was so tall that the first time I hid there no one ever thought to look up. They never knew where I was until I'd silently tagged them all and the game was over.

The only spot that was better than the fig tree was found by our neighbor to our right. His name was Ted. Without our knowledge, Ted bought a laser gun for himself and patiently waited one evening inside his home for us to begin to play. Suddenly all our targets began to buzz. We thought there had been some kind of electronic disturbance in the universe. We were lighting up like we were all radioactive, yet no one was shooting! It turned out to be Ted who had been picking off both teams one-by-one from behind the window inside his darkened kitchen. We never knew what hit us until Ted burst through his back door, laser gun in hand, laughing like a hyena. We nearly banned him from all future games!

One memorable Saturday night we had lots of company over for dinner. After the meal the adults were talking and laughing around the table but the kids and I had something better to do. As darkness fell, another dad and I excused ourselves to *supervise* the children who were impatiently waiting for us to play Laser Tag.

There they all were, the usual suspects; Ted from next door, Ben's high school friends, Megan's younger playmates who were visiting with their parents, and a few neighborhood kids. We fielded two teams of eight players each. Sixteen ball-cap-wearing night prowlers fully locked, loaded and lighted. The game had us all "hyped." We could feel the adrenaline begin to pump as we imagined ourselves to be Han Solo or Princess Leah fighting off the Evil Empire.

This night was epic! When one team won the first round, the losing team insisted we play the best out of three rounds, which soon turned into the three out of five, which advanced to five out of seven. The game didn't get old—it just got more intense as we refined our hiding and *tagging* skills. I think we were on our way to the best of seven out of nine games when we were all startled by a loud noise that projected like thunder from behind our backyard fence.

Everyone INSTANTLY FROZE in the darkened silence. It was a human voice, an unfamiliar voice, a voice we had never heard before! It was a low, commanding, smoldering voice. It was *The Phantom of the Okra!* I faced the fence full-on to put myself between the imminent threat and the children.

"You, sir"—Freda Fay said with a disdain that made me think she didn't really mean the "sir" part. "You, sir, do you know what time it is?"

It was a very good question. I didn't know what time it was. I thought it might be a little after 9:00—but I had the feeling that I was about to find out for sure. Peering through one of the slats in the tall fence, I saw an eye and a nose and part of a mouth. Freda Fay continued, and I not only heard but felt the full volume of her disgust.

"It's nearly 1:00 in the morning!"

I'm not really sure what Freda Fay said after that but there was a

LOT more! I'm sure what followed had something to do with bothering the whole neighborhood and being a bad model for children and, in general, being an inconsiderate neighbor. Somewhere in there, there might also have been a line about being ashamed of myself. I was relieved that she didn't mention my bad example as a pastor (she probably didn't know I was a pastor), and for this I was thankful. I wanted to take my flashing red hat off but I felt it might be disrespectful to interrupt her with my movement as she yelled at me.

It was embarrassing. As she shouted at me, I saw fifteen motionless images scattered in the shadows; their blinking ball caps put silent exclamation points on each of her clipped sentences.

For a fleeting moment I thought to myself, *Doesn't this old curmudgeon know how to have fun? Has she no sense of adventure?* But then I pressed the light on my watch. She was right: it was well after midnight! We had been so involved in the game that we had not noticed we had played into the *wee hours* of the next day. The whole neighborhood must have been tossing in their beds asking, *When is this deafening combat going to be over?*

When Freda Fay was done with us, we beat a hasty retreat to our family room inside the house. The news of how our *cease-fire* had come about pretty much ended the party for everyone.

I didn't sleep much that night. I had to work through the self-justification. After all, I was just being a good father having fun with my kids. On the other hand I was also an adult having so much fun that I had acted like an immature child. I had disregarded sleeping neighbors and waiting parents who must have wondered where their children were. I wondered how I was going to face my neighbor across the backyard fence in the light of day.

I knew what I had to do.

I stopped by the market on the way home from church the next day. I bought a little bouquet of flowers in a basket and I attached a note.

Dear Freda Fay,

    I am so sorry for keeping you, and perhaps others in the neighborhood, awake last night. We were having so much fun that I lost total track of time. We will try very hard to be mindful of the clock when having fun in the future.

I signed the apology and left the basket of flowers on her front door (I couldn't muster the courage to face her). I didn't see her until the next day.

When I did see her from our dining room window, she was working in her garden. I steeled myself to go into the yard and face the music. I walked up to the fence and spoke through well-worn slats— after all, she'd already broken the ice by *speaking* first!

"Freda Fay," I said. "I'm so sorry for the other night."

She was several feet back from the fence in the middle of her yard. I remember that she took her wide-brimmed gardening hat off before she spoke. From the distance between the slats I could see her full face in the sunlight; it was emotionless. She came closer. I braced myself! She looked me in the eye between the slats and said these exact words that I have remembered for over thirty years.

"How can I be angry with a guy who brings me flowers?"

Whew! Things changed after that—*The Phantom of the Okra* became our newly-named neighbor, Freda Fay. She no longer darted quickly between the fence slats. Now she would pause, wait to catch our eye, and cheerfully greet us.

"Hi, how are you doing today?"

Shortly after that, she invited my daughter to her backyard to help her plant her garden. This was an activity they regularly shared together thereafter. A few times Megan was invited into her home to view some special treasure, and when Freda Fay went on vacation, we were entrusted with feeding the fish in her prized koi pond.

It's funny how apologies work—once I'd completed mine in person that Sunday—Freda Fay asked me to pardon her for being "a little too upset at a family that had just lost track of time because they were having so much fun." We never spoke of Laser Tag again.

Over the years I've had to say "I'm sorry" more times than I can remember. I have often suffered from poor judgment. Sometimes I've done the wrong thing; many times I've just failed to do the right thing. Often I've had to work through being too defensive when I was justly criticized.

When all is said and done, I've found there is nothing so freeing as facing a person you've wronged with the simple words, "I'm sorry, I'll try to do better." If your apology is sincere, most of the time folks feel better about you. Sometimes, they even feel better about themselves.

1 0

ANGELS AMONG US

Let mutual love continue.

 Do not neglect to show hospitality to strangers, for by doing that some have entertained angels without knowing it.

    HEBREWS 13:1–2

If there was ever an angel on earth it was Nancy Wilson. Nancy was an expressive blue-eyed, blond-haired cherub with a smile that lit up the room. Her contagious laugh would have charmed Attila the Hun into having a good day.

Nancy was a member of our church youth group and I was her pastor and her team's driver for the "Back-to-School Scavenger Hunt." The youth group had been divided into team cars filled with enthusiastic middle schoolers. We had a time limit and a list of tasks to accomplish before returning to the church for prizes and dinner.

The tasks didn't seem that difficult—it was the time factor that provided the challenge. The team that got all five things AND got back first would win the prize. The items on the list were:

1. Dented can of food from Bell Market;
2. Blank patient wristband from Sequoia Hospital;
3. Cardboard coffee sleeve from the Plantation Coffee Roastery;
4. Clothes hanger from the local dry cleaner—and
5. Signature of a gas station customer who allows one of your team to fill their tank with gas.

At the sound of "GO!" five kids piled into my Ford and we headed for Bell Market, planning the rest of our strategy on the way. My carload of youthful extroverts was filled with energy and we quickly captured the first four items on the list.

As we drove I kept reminding the team that our chances of winning didn't just depend on getting all five items, but on doing it faster than anyone else!

As the car rolled to our last stop at a gas station, Nancy bolted from the car to get a head start. She had been listening intently to my counsel about the time remaining and she wasn't going to waste a moment. She headed straight for the fuel pumps.

As I opened my car door to cheer her on, I looked toward the young family in a white Honda where I thought she was headed. Since they were all still in their car, Nancy decided to save time by veering off toward the next customer instead. He was a large, long-haired, heavily bearded man who had just swung his leg off the saddle of his gigantic Harley-Davidson. Other than his size, his long hair, and the immensity of his black chopper, there was only one other distinctive feature about him. He wore a heavy leather jacket with a gold wing in the middle of the back. Printed above the wing, in bold capital letters, was the name of his motorcycle gang, "HELLS ANGELS."

By the time I got out of my car, Nancy was already approaching the biker. I could hear her excited voice from about 20 feet away.

"Hi sir, I'm on a scavenger hunt with my church youth group. That's my pastor over there." She waved and pointed at me. I smiled with a glazed look of panic on my face and awkwardly waved back. The burly biker stared at me—he did not wave!

Nancy continued, "Can I—please, please, please—fill up your motorcycle with gas to help us win the contest?"

Nancy did not know that the United States (and Canadian) Departments of Justice considered the "HELLS ANGELS" an organized crime syndicate. She wasn't aware that today the *Web* says their motto is, "When we do right, nobody remembers. When we do wrong, nobody forgets." (Sounds a little defensive for a club motto, don't you think?)

It was too late to pull Nancy aside and whisper, *Let's ask this nice young family if we can fill their tank instead (because they probably aren't involved in drug trafficking, robbery, and extortion!)*

As the shaggy-haired man sized me up, I could see nothing but his dark squinty eyes peering at me above a massive Fu Manchu moustache. He looked at Nancy, then back at me, then back at Nancy again—a faint smile began to percolate beneath his forestlike beard.

"Sure, I guess so," he said, motioning Nancy toward his motorcycle.

I exhaled in a sigh of tentative relief.

"That's the gas cap on top—unscrew it," he said.

I was now bravely praying from behind a gas pump several feet away.

The biker turned his back on me to pay attention to Nancy and his bike. As he pivoted, I noticed two other small patches on the back of his jacket. One read "Oakland"; the other read "Sergeant at Arms." This was a pastoral circumstance for which seminary had not prepared me —I decided to let Nancy handle it!

It was clear that she had never filled a gas tank before in her life. Still she had all the eagerness of any middle schooler to try something new, whether she knew how or not.

Nancy's outlaw had now forgotten all about me and was taking on a gentle fatherly manner with his enthusiastic newfound junior high cheerleader friend.

She unscrewed the cap and laid it on top of the gas tank.

He quickly plucked the cap from its resting place on the shiny tank top. Shaking his finger tenderly at her, he said softly, "You don't want to scratch it."

He handed her the nozzle and told her to put it in the tank just above skull decal!

"Pull the trigger," he said.

"This is fun! Thank you!" she giggled.

Peeking out from behind the pump, I could see the corners of his moustache rising in a telltale grin beneath the overgrowth; he was enjoying this.

It took only a few seconds to fill the tank. As the gas neared the top of the tank, he asked her to take the nozzle out carefully. He neglected to tell her to let go of the "trigger" before doing so!

As Nancy pulled out the nozzle, gas poured all over the shiny black fuel tank. The biker quickly put his hand over Nancy's and stopped the flow. He grabbed a nearby paper towel and began to soak up the gasoline from his pride and joy.

"Sorry," she said.

He silently kept grabbing paper towels and doing damage control.

Oblivious to the hazardous waste dump she'd initiated, Nancy continued talking.

"Will you sign our list to prove I filled your tank? My pastor has it."

The *Viking* grunted and looked back at me again without smiling. I timidly approached the bike and began to lay the pen and paper on the fuselage.

"NOT on the gas tank!" he bellowed.

He grabbed the pen and paper from my hands and signed, giving me a cold hard stare that said, *If this little girl wasn't here, I'd* ... then he smiled at Nancy, pulled another towel from the dispenser, and continued mopping his *ride*.

"Goodbye" she said, giving him a quick hug.

"And thank you VERY, VERY MUCH!"

The biker watched her get back into my car. She leaned out the open window and waved goodbye one last time. The dark rider paused from cleaning his mucky motorcycle. He looked first to his left, and then to his right (no one else was watching). He then lifted his gas-soaked hand and waved at Nancy. His accompanying grin began to grow so broad that I could actually see a few of his teeth beneath the rangy jungle of beard.

I wanted the children to win the contest—so I drove out of that gas station as fast as I could! I was also hoping NOT to spend the rest of the week recovering in the hospital. I kept looking in the rearview mirror to be sure we didn't have a motorcycle escort all the way back to the church.

To this day, I get butterflies in my stomach when a motorcycle overtakes me by surprise on the freeway. My grip on the wheel tightens at the startling roar and I wish, just for an instant, that Nancy were still in the passenger seat of my car—just in case! I always look to see if the rider is a "HELLS ANGEL"—from Oakland!

In contrast, Nancy, now the mother of three boys, has a different reaction. I contacted her and she wrote back saying, "I do recall this gentleman being kind and gracious…. Since then, I've always had a warm feeling when I see 'HELLS ANGELS' on the back of a motorcyclist's jacket. The phrase 'You can't judge a book by its cover' comes to mind."

A lot of God's children respond to pain in their lives by forming scar tissue over His image. They put on a tough shield to protect themselves but even then, if you treat them with respect, *you mostly get back what you give.* Even if people wear outward signs that suggest other affiliations, God's monogram is stamped deep into EVERY human heart.

Jesus said, *"Do to others what you would have them do to you…."*[1] He meant for us to treat others with kindness, respect, and helpfulness regardless of a person's clothing, color, accent, or religion. He taught that we are all God's children and therefore brothers and sisters because in the deepest places we ALL bear the image of our Father.

Neither Nancy nor I remember who won the "Back-to-School Scavenger Hunt." What we do remember is that I stood fearfully gawking in a gas station at a HELLS ANGEL; Nancy, unmindful of outward appearances, connected with a man she assumed to be a kind stranger. I read the outward signs and took the prejudicial shortcut (he sensed it), Nancy saw an approachable human being created in the image of God (he sensed that too)!

The whole encounter with the Hell's Angel lasted no more than five minutes, yet Nancy and I still remember it more than three decades later.

If WE remember, I wonder if he still remembers. I wonder if he thinks that he met an angel that day too; one that overfilled his tank with gas and his heart with a touch of unmerited affection. It wouldn't surprise me if Jesus was on a scavenger hunt that day beginning to collect a new recruit. Perhaps God was sending a message in that moment years ago through an angelic little girl—a message to a renegade—a renegade not so different from you and me.

The Bible gives us another reason to treat people respectfully: *"Do not neglect to show hospitality to strangers, for by doing that some have entertained angels without knowing it."*[2] In this verse, the Greek word that is used for "angel" is the same common word that is translated elsewhere in the Bible as "messenger." I guess the biblical writers thought the difference between an angel and a messenger was too close to call—so do I.

11

THE CHEER OF THE CLOUD

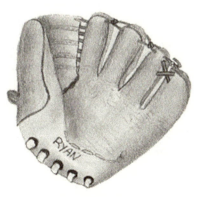

Therefore, since we are surrounded by so great a cloud of witnesses, let us also lay aside every weight and the sin that clings so closely,

And let us run with perseverance the race that is set before us,

Looking to Jesus the pioneer and perfector of our faith….

HEBREWS 12:1–2A

It all began with Nadine Cluny, a tall, sun-tanned brunette. I'll never forget how beautiful she looked as her kind brown eyes met mine. Nadine came along at a particularly vulnerable time in my life; a time when my self-worth was in question. I felt stupid, helpless, and vulnerable as a crowd began to encircle me. I sat huddled on the ground in tears—the worst thing that I could imagine had happened—my shoe had come untied!

I was five years old and burning with shame as I sat on the kindergarten play yard. What if the other kids found out I didn't know how to tie a bow?

It was then that Nadine Cluny came into my life. She appeared as an angel of mercy. She didn't think I was stupid; she didn't think I was a failure. She didn't even ask why I was crying. She just saw me in need on the ground and she wanted to do something to make me feel better. As the sunshine backlit her burnished curls, Nadine Cluny, though only five years old herself, knelt to the ground beside me.

"It's okay. Don't cry," she said. Then taking my undone laces in her hands, she quietly tied them and smiled.

Lots of people have helped and encouraged me since Nadine, but outside of my immediate family she is my first memory of a gentle voice from the crowd who came to my rescue. You can never underestimate the power of a cheer from a friend in the crowd. One voice can make a difference!

Some years ago, the guys in my church asked me to join their city league softball team. I took my place at second base, proudly wearing the team's yellow and black jersey which displayed our corresponding name—*Killer Bees*.

There is one game that I have remembered in detail for many years. It was one of those damp San Francisco fog-cooled evenings under the city park lights. The stands were full of families. The game got off to a fast start when our associate pastor, Skip Murphy, who played left field, hit a towering homerun with the bases loaded, giving us a four-run lead.

Our lead held up for several innings until I let the team down. I made two errors in a row. The first was a hard hit grounder that went embarrassingly right between my legs. I was watching where I was going to throw the ball instead of watching the ball all the way into my glove. I tried to shake it off.

Great ball players make an error and then hope for the next ball to be hit to them so they can redeem themselves and get back in the game—I'm not a great ball player! Instead, my mind was replaying my error in *technicolor* and *slow-mo*. My face felt flushed with embarrassment. I wanted out of the game.

Suddenly my self-consciousness was interrupted by the ping of the aluminum bat. I looked up just in time to see something small and white careening through space at hyperspeed. Unless I moved my head (and pretty fast), it was going to be permanently displaced. I jerked to the side and threw my glove up in self-defense. The ball careened off my glove—it was awkward!

For the second time, I wasn't paying attention; my head was in my previous error, not in the game. Their next batter drove it over the fence and we now led by the slim margin of only one run.

To play it safe with our lead, the coach moved me to right field for the rest of the game where it was less likely I would do further damage to the team. Right field was a place where I could feel embarrassed and clumsy all by myself away from the crowd. (You know a person could die in right field in some games and not be found until the next time they cut the grass—and that night—that would have been okay with me!)

You don't have to have played baseball to know what it's like out there in right field. Right field is that lonesome place where, were it not for the heckling, you might feel totally abandoned. Unlike the player who is put there because he's a great hitter, I was there because I was the team's worst fielder. For me, it felt like a place of public humiliation, a place where you feel like you are dying naked publically. Even if you've never picked up a baseball glove, you know what right field feels like.

We still led by one run in the final inning of the game. I had gone unchallenged in right field and was glad of it! It was then that I noticed that their batters were squaring their shoulders to hit the ball to right field. It wasn't enough that my two errors gave them new life earlier— now they were picking on me to test the weak link with their *last ups* and their final chance. I thought to myself, *Why am I even playing ball? Is this fun?*

Fortunately their next batter grounded out, the next popped up for the second out. The third batter hit a line drive between shortstop and second base. Now their *heavy hitter* was up with two outs and a man on base. The potential winning run was standing at the plate. He was looking at me and swinging his bat in the direction of the fence directly behind me. Our coach raised both arms from the dugout and with his open palms he *pushed* me deep toward the fence.

I began to pray, *Lord, please don't let him hit me another ball.* (I'd had enough for one night!)

At that exact moment my prayer was interrupted by a sharp sound 150 feet away. It was the sound of a fly ball launching off a Louisville Slugger. I had an immediate revelation—God was not going to answer my prayer the way I wanted Him to. For me, this was a moment frozen in time; I still see it clearly. There it was—a short fly ball too deep for the second baseman but too shallow for me to reach from deep right field.

I didn't feel like running, but I had to run. No one else could get to the ball and I was the only right fielder playing at that moment! My stomach was churning, it was saying—*Wonderful, another chance to fail!*

A suffocating silence fell over the crowd. Everyone in the stands and everyone now standing in the dugouts held their breath. The ball was descending into *no-man's land,* too far from me for an easy catch, yet close enough to me that if I didn't catch it on a short hop, it was sure to roll beyond me.

Should I dive for it or catch it on the bounce? This thought had barely registered in my brain when a loud, deep voice rang out above the crystal-clear silence. The voice pealed like a thunder roll from heaven. There was no timidity, no doubt, and no question in this voice. Everyone in the ballpark heard it. It was Skip Murphy's voice—clear, confident, reassuring—"Go for it, Eddie!"

His words took hold and my indecisive steps gained strength. My eyes fixed on the plummeting ball and everything went into slow motion as I stretched out my left foot, bent as low as I could, and put my glove an inch above the grass in front of my stride. The lunge was followed by a gangly somersault roll in the grass. When I finally flopped to a sitting stop with my legs in front of me, I opened my glove and peered inside—the ball was there! I had made the *shoestring catch* of my life. Out number three! Game over! Pizza time!

Left on my own, I'd have never made that catch. It was a cheer from a friend in the *crowd* that gave me the courage to keep going!

There have, of course, been other cheering voices in my life. I've heard cheers from family, friends, youth leaders, and teachers. Some of these voices were heard over the phone, some spoke through notes, some challenged me in a counselor's office, and some prayed over me in small groups. These voices were not just spectators in the wings; they were fans in my stands. Everyone falls into a slump now and then; no one bats or catches 100 percent of the balls that come their way. A cheer from the crowd can make a powerful difference!

My son, Ben—former batboy for the *Killer Bees*—is a fantastic dad and a great Little League coach. At the end of one of his games he walked from the dugout to the bleachers and gave me a big bear hug.

"Dad, it means a lot to see you over here in the stands and to hear you cheering us on."

I got to thinking, *I don't believe anyone ever makes a catch, finishes a race, or becomes a follower of Jesus without a positive voice from the crowd cheering them on.*

If you've ever heard from a Nadine or a Skip—you know what I'm talking about. God values a cheering voice so much that the Bible tells us that even when *our game* is over, we will still be standing tall—and cheering from the *"cloud."* [1] Being a cheerleader Himself—God wants us to be one too!

12

KEEPING THE BIRDS FROM THEIR MISSION

No temptation has seized you except what is common to man.

And God is faithful; he will not let you be tempted beyond what you can bear.

But when you are tempted, he will also provide a way out so that you can stand up under it.

I CORINTHIANS 10:13 NIV

The swallows that mysteriously descended on *Mission San Juan Capistrano* every March 19 for a century haven't returned for many years now—I'm pretty sure it's my fault!

I've never hated birds, but I haven't always loved them either. I've seen blue jays swoop onto picnic tables and steal the lunches of small children.

Once, I somehow became the archenemy of a mockingbird. Each day as I jogged beneath his tree, he swooped down on my head as though I was the *Death Star* and he was Luke Skywalker. The *Force* was so strong in him that eventually I had to change my jogging path.

On another occasion as I walked across a vacant stadium parking lot, a flock of crows swooped at me repeatedly until I finally reached the safety of my car 100 yards away. I hadn't done a thing to them; it was unnerving. I couldn't help but think of that old Alfred Hitchcock movie where the birds all join forces and begin attacking humans. [1] Sometimes our feathered *friends* don't act like it!

Some years ago I was appointed the executive director of a luxurious senior living community in a town just a little north of San Juan Capistrano. At about that same time, there were workers who cleared away the cliff swallow nests from the walls of the mission to do some repair work.

The architecture of the brand-new senior apartment building was the classic Spanish style, similar to the *San Juan Mission*. My new community had a rough-textured, adobe-colored finish with a massive red tile roof. It was a large multistoried structure that, like the *Capistrano Mission,* had towering high walls. It was perhaps 30 miles away from the mission, but that's not really far "as the crow flies"—it's not far at all as the swallow flies.

San Juan Capistrano's cliff swallows fly 12,000 miles a year! They winter in Argentina and return here around March 19, *St. Joseph's Day*, to build (and then annually return to) their nests for spring and summer.

We had run the final *punch list* to finish all the construction on the senior living community. It had a fitness room, a large game room, a spa, and pool. It even had a bistro filled with the aroma of freshly baked chocolate chip cookies and coffee. There was a gorgeous dining room with a theater kitchen complete with a warm glowing pizza oven that exuded an old-world atmosphere. There was a second separate dining room for those who needed physical assistance and a third exquisite private dining room for families to celebrate special occasions with residents.

We began moving new residents into the premium apartments the day we opened. All was going beautifully. Word was traveling fast; we were the brightest and best senior living community for miles around. Just as important to me, we were giving birth to a community of caring; a safe place that celebrated health and wellness and a passion for life at any age.

The executives at corporate headquarters were ecstatic. We were filling the building way ahead of schedule. A community that filled faster than expected meant both quicker and higher profits. My boss was happy, the residents were happy, and I was happy.

That all changed on March 19, *St. Joseph's Day*, the day of the swallows' traditional return to *The Great Stone Church* at Mission San Juan Capistrano.

When I opened the dark oak front door of the *Grand Lobby* that morning, ready for another day of touring delighted new customers, I was met by a resident who was living on the top floor of the building.

"Hello Margaret, how are you this morning?"

"Not very good," she responded. "I have bird droppings all over my patio!"

"Really," I said, "Well, let's go take a look at what can be done about that."

I saw Bill, our maintenance man, in the hall as we headed to her apartment. I motioned for him to join us and bring something to help us sweep up the mess.

Margaret wasn't kidding. When we opened the sliding glass door to her balcony, it looked as though her patio railings, furniture, and deck had been hit by a heavy powdering of snow—NOT the good kind! This was not just a light skirmish; this was an avalanche of fowl doings.

Bill came out to the terrace and noticed something neither Margaret nor I had seen. There were little birds darting back and forth trying to stick tiny particles to the outside walls just under the over-hanging tile roof.

We tried discouraging them with a broom, being careful not to hit the birds or step in something! When we did this, the birds would simply move to another patio a few apartments away and begin again. When we moved down the hall and shooed them from that apartment, they simply returned to the original one and began building again. There were too many birds and not enough brooms.

Soon, what began as a moderate dusting was becoming a bird bliz-zard. The first birds had evidently only been the scouts. As we looked beyond the patio roof, there were hundreds of birds coming from the south and circling in the sky above my beautiful, freshly-finished community.

I told Bill to keep swinging a broom while I returned to my office to call for help. When I entered the lobby again downstairs, I was greeted by an angry mob. These previously pleasant residents were demanding I do something about THEIR patios. It seems it was not just the uppermost floor that was under aerial attack. Now the collateral damage was drifting to the verandas of the residents on the lower floors!

I began to see senior citizens armed with brooms marauding through the building like rogue gangs. Occasionally, they could be seen across the courtyard on their patios poking at the dive-bombing birds. One resident put down her broom, stood on her patio chair, and carefully removed her hanging bird feeder—it didn't help!

Though it was probably 70 degrees out, the entire building was beginning to clatter with the effects of this *tropical snowstorm*. It was an impossible game of *broom tag* where the humans were always *it* and the birds never got tagged.

My residents who were in their *golden years* were now on *red alert*. Bits of nest and mud and bird *debris* drifted all over our once peaceful and pristine community like a blizzard. Though the evidence of bird presence was everywhere, the swallows preferred the higher floors with impressive balconies and expensive views. This meant the higher your floor, the steeper your rent, the deeper your *snowpack*.

Bolting the door to my office behind me, I called the Health Department and the Humane Society. The Health Department told me that the nesting materials the birds were bringing from the local pastures and stables could be hazardous to the elderly.

"Birds can carry up to sixty known diseases including the *E. coli Virus*," they said.

The Humane Society had no better news. I can still hear the ominous voice at the other end of the phone.

"These birds are protected by law, and once a swallow has built a nest on the building it cannot be removed. You can be fined up to five hundred dollars and given six months in jail FOR EACH nest you remove!" *What a fine St. Joseph's Day this was turning out to be!*

Since government institutions proved little help, I called our corporate office. True to corporate offices everywhere, they offered a penetrating glimpse into the obvious. They said, (and I quote), "Then don't let them build nests!"

My bosses neglected to suggest just how I might keep the birds from accomplishing their mission. I had one maintenance man, over thirty top-floor balconies, and nearly a thousand birds. But then if you've ever worked for corporate, you know that they are responsible for policy—YOU are responsible for implementation!

I called Bill on his walkie-talkie from my office bunker and told him to go to the hardware store and buy the most powerful pressure sprayer he could find. Money was no object—speed was the only thing that would keep us out of jail!

Before long Bill returned equipped with a power washer. Aiming up from the courtyard he sprayed water all the way to the roofline of the building. These were only warning shots for the birds but once they were gone he aimed to dislodge the budding nests.

He walked from one end of the very long building to the other. As the birds relocated, he would go back and start all over again. The pace had to be constant; not one single nest could be completed—my job, not to mention *my freedom*—depended on it!

The *armed sentry duty* continued for days with staff members slipping into Bill's yellow nor'easter hat, slicker, and pants whenever he needed a break. Everyone who took a turn had to be trained on how to keep from hurting the birds while destroying the nests before they were completed.

Some of the line staff thought this was funny but the managers knew that what hung in the balance if these homesteaders were tolerated was not just dirty patios. It could mean disease, an empty new building, loss of jobs, fines, and, of most concern to me, *hard time* in the county jail.

Cliff swallows are persistent! The siege went on from dawn to dusk for days. The building had the feel of an aviary with a constant mist saturating the air and birds fluttering overhead everywhere! In addition to being the guy responsible for luring the swallows from Capistrano, I'm likely responsible for the water shortage in California as well.

By the third week, the birds were gone. All it took was two weeks of a high-pressure hose and one week of installing an almost invisible netting under the eaves of the roof—all for a mere $30,000.

Martin Luther is attributed a quote that has ever since had special meaning for me, "You can't keep the birds from flying over your head but you can keep them from building a nest in your hair!"[2]

Luther wasn't really talking about birds but about the tiny winged temptations that swoop in almost unnoticed at first into all our lives. Luther knew that once you begin giving yourself small permissions to do the wrong thing, the temptation begins to lay eggs and produce offspring at an extraordinary rate—year-after-year-after year! It's better to sweep away the first signs of nesting when you can than risk eventually having to "pay the fine and do the time."

The *temple* God has given us is first class. It is the wise person who takes a few moments each day to check the nooks and crannies for the beginnings of *bird nests*. A little power spraying today can eliminate a big mess tomorrow.

13

UNREST IN THE REST HOME

Put away from you all bitterness and wrath and anger and wrangling and slander, together with all malice, and be kind to one another, tenderhearted, forgiving one another, as God in Christ has forgiven you.

EPHESIANS 4:31–32

Adversity is unavoidable. No one gets through life without being pushed, hit, teased, or worse. When someone puts a dagger in your back, you remember the wound.

Some victims pull that painful dagger out, and from that moment forward use it to strike others first. Others, having been wounded, adopt the dagger like a doctor's scalpel and use their experience to promote healing, kindness, tenderness, and forgiveness. A painful experience is a two-edged sword in our hands; we decide to use it to hurt or to heal.

A framed certificate hangs high on the wall of my study at home. There is an inscription and a memento mounted in the glass frame. It was given to me as a gift by some of the people with whom I once worked. The inscription reads:

In Memory of Your Bravery
The Unnamed Resident Debacle
Apartment 22

Each time my eyes wander up the wall, I chuckle as I read that plaque—but it is a nervous chuckle. The "Unnamed Resident Debacle" could have been my last debacle. Fortunately, I've lived to debacle several more times since then.

I should have known that George, "the unnamed resident," was trouble the first time I interviewed him to be a resident in my new senior living community. He was filled with an excessive bravado that betrayed that something was not quite right beneath the surface. A retired lawyer with a distinguished military career, George had earned both scars and honors in the Korean War. I knew something in him was a little *off*, but as he signed the contract to move in, I avoided any possible discord and kept my questions to myself—I love to avoid conflict. I wanted to fill the apartment complex, and I wanted to give this veteran a comfortable place to live in his final years.

I had no idea how much hurt and anger brewed inside of George. He never talked about his pain, but it wasn't long before his gruff edges began to annoy those around him. Anger came about as naturally to George as chewing gum. He was quick to dish out bitterness and wrath from the boiling kettle of hurt that simmered inside him. Sometimes *hurt people hurt people*. They give what they got.

It wasn't long before the people at George's dinner table began to tire of his profanity (which he had never used in my presence). Next, residents told me that he was being vulgar and rude to the young high school girl who served their table at the evening meal.

I confirmed his bad behavior with the student server and then I spoke to George about it—twice! The second time I told him clearly that if there was a third incident he would have to leave. Each time he seemed shocked that people thought him offensive. He promised me it would not happen again—both times!

The straw that broke the camel's back came when one of our residents came to into my office and said, "My wife and I are moving out if George stays!"

This is just the kind of thing a manager who likes to avoid conflict loves to hear! I could hardly believe it as the husband told me that his wife had been in the laundry room the day before when George had accosted her. He had yelled at her for monopolizing the dryers and then threatened her, "The next time you use more than one dryer, I'm going to empty your clothes from it and stuff YOU inside it!"

This was not the spirit of kindness that I was trying to cultivate in the community. There was no need to warn George again. Though I love to avoid conflict, I called my boss at corporate headquarters and he agreed that it was time for action.

I was told to ask George to come to my office and to have my business manager present when I served the thirty-day eviction notice—I, however, had a better idea!

George had not seemed upset when I had talked to him before about his behavior. I thought to myself, *I'll just go to his apartment and explain things nonconfrontationally. George will be disappointed but he will understand. We'll handle this like two mature adults.*

I made an appointment to see him in his apartment the following day.

As I entered his apartment the next day, I noticed the military memorabilia. There was a picture of his old Army Ranger unit on the bookshelf. A medal with a purple ribbon hung in a frame on the wall beside his desk. On the desk sat a red, white, and blue coffee mug and a largish letter opener that resembled a military bayonet.

I hated to tell a war hero he had to leave, but George's vulgarity and threats could not be tolerated. My community had to be civil and safe for all the residents and staff.

George invited me to sit in a chair in his living room. He then settled in the sofa across from me.

He was lean and healthy for a seventy-five-year-old man; I was in my late fifties.

I handed him the eviction notice and began to quietly express my regret.

"George, I tried to tell you this day might come."

George stood up as he read the final paragraph. His face was beet-red. I could tell something good was NOT about to happen!

I was about halfway up out of my chair to stand with him when all of a sudden it felt like the ceiling had caved in on me. I literally didn't know what had hit me.

Then I put two and two together. I realized that while I was getting up staring at the floor and searching for nonconfrontational words, George had clobbered me with a right-handed *haymaker punch* to the side of my face!

The punch didn't hurt—George was seventy-five—but the whip-lash sent my glasses flying across the room (I wasn't sure where). Stunned, I took my eyes off George to pay serious attention to finding my glasses quickly. George took advantage of the moment with a left-handed, follow-up punch to the other side of my face. In addition to being a conflict avoider, I'm evidently a slow learner!

For a guy who doesn't like conflict, I was in a very difficult position. First I was being physically attacked by a seventy-five-year-old battle veteran—second, I couldn't see him very well.

Finally, I began to reason that if I kept looking for my glasses rather than paying attention to George, I was probably going to get hit again. I looked up through blurry vision at George just in time to see him reach toward his desk and pick up the bayonet-shaped letter opener. He came toward me with a thrusting motion. Through his grit-ted teeth I heard these very distinct words.

"I'm going to kill you!"

As I said—for a guy who doesn't like conflict, I was in a very difficult situation.

Oddly, I wasn't scared. I was shocked. I was thinking to myself, *Is this really happening? Am I really in hand-to-hand combat with one of my residents?*

We sparred around his living room like two prize fighters. He thrust the point of the letter opener at me several times as I tried to see him clearly enough to grab his wrist. For a moment I considered trying to trip him but I still had the presence of mind to imagine the head-lines that might appear in the next day's newspaper: ***REST HOME MANAGER ABUSES ELDERLY WAR HERO!***

I knew I had to end this battle without hurting George. I wanted to end it without becoming another trophy on his wall!

After several bobs and weaves, I managed to clamp my hand around George's wrist. (I think he'd worn himself out lunging at me. This had to be more aerobic exercise than he'd had for years.)

Once I had a firm grip on him, George spoke, "Okay, just let go of my wrist and I'll stop."

By now I had learned that trusting George was probably NOT a good idea! I carefully peeled the weapon from his hand and moved him toward his sofa, again hoping he was not about to die from a heart attack.

I pulled my cell phone from my pocket and called my business manager downstairs. Kathleen knew I'd gone up to serve George the eviction notice.

"How's it going?" she said.

"Well, it could have gone better," I responded.

George was still seething and muttering in the background as he stood in front of the sofa. Kathleen could hear him in the background as he announced, "So, you've taken my knife—I suppose now you're going to take my gun too?"

She immediately hung up on me—and called 911!

Meanwhile upstairs in the apartment, I sat George down on the sofa again and tried to calm him. (I made sure I was sitting out of haymaker range.)

We talked quietly until there was a loud knock on the door. I opened it to see two police officers with hands on their guns. I explained to them what happened. George agreed, offering no objections except that he didn't think it was fair of me to evict him.

The police asked if he had a gun. He said he had only said that to scare me—IT WORKED!

The police put George's hands behind his back. They dug out a long overcoat from his closet and put it over his shoulders to camouflage the cuffs. I watched as they walked him down the long hallway to a back door and their squad car. The officers told me that he would likely make bail and be back before morning!

I called our corporate office and they told me that under no circumstances was it legal for me to go through his private apartment looking for a gun! This time I really did have a better idea! I hung up the phone and went through every drawer, box, and piece of furniture in George's apartment. I figured I'd rather be guilty of disturbing George's property than dead from his artillery.

Thankfully, there was no gun!

I didn't go home that night. I slept in my office. About 2:30 AM, I heard a car in the driveway. I watched from between the slats in my window blinds as George and his son went up to his apartment.

The next morning George marched into my office.

"I'm going to move out of this dump, but I'm going to take as long as I want...."

I interrupted him. I told him to sit down and this time I asked my office manager to join us! I looked George in the eye, and for a guy who doesn't like conflict, Kathleen said I did okay.

"George, I want you out of this place in seven days. I don't care where you go but if on the eighth day you are not completely out, I am going to press charges for assault and attempted murder."

That was the last thing I said to George. He was completely out of the building in five days. The next January at our annual Executive Directors Conference, I was asked to do a short training seminar for all the managers in the company on *HOW NOT TO SERVE AN EVICTION NOTICE!*

My father's first name was Weldon. He often told people his name was a biblical one. When they scratched their heads, he would quote it directly from the Scriptures, *"Well done, thou good and faithful servant."* [1]

Dad's middle name was George. He too had experienced a lot of pain in his life and he could have easily allowed it to turn him into a bitter and angry person. His mother died when he was only four. Unable to care for his sons, his alcoholic father sent him and his brothers to an orphanage. One day when Dad was about six years old, the headmaster of the orphanage asked the boys to dress in suits and ties for a trolley car ride. They imagined they were going somewhere exciting like the circus; instead, they were taken to their father's funeral. Dad's father had been hit by a train. It was rumored that alcohol had been involved.

Dad often talked to me about his childhood and youth. It was clear that he learned most of his lessons about life through *the school of hard knocks*. The amazing thing was that when he told the stories, sad as the circumstances were, there was always laughter. Dad made a brutal orphanage seem like fun. Never once as he repeated the stories of beatings with a belt and exploitation by the older children did I ever sense hatred in him for those who'd abused him. He would close every story with a smile and these amazing words, "They didn't know any better."

My dad eagerly excused bad behavior in others because of the pain they'd experienced, but he never allowed his own pain to become an excuse for behaving badly. Dad chose in his own way to say what Jesus said on the cross, *"Father, forgive them; for they do not know what they are doing."*[2]

Somewhere along his thorny path to adulthood, God touched my dad's wounded heart with grace. It was hard to tell where the hand of mercy had first touched him because all his memories of mistreatment now seemed bathed in clemency. Whatever the moment of redemption was, from that day on Dad began to exchange bitterness for kindness, wrath for tenderheartedness, and anger for forgiveness. I never heard him slander or wrangle on about anyone, but I often heard him forgive.

Sometimes *hurt people hurt people*—sometimes, but not always! Dad faced the cutting memories and decided the mean people in his life were to be pitied. Rather than giving hurt for hurt, he forgave as he'd been forgiven. His own wounds healed without a trace of visible scar tissue.

The cross is the difference between these two men who shared the same name. Once my dad had opened his wounds before the cross of Jesus, his own wounds seemed insignificant (even laughable) by comparison.

When you take a good look at a cross, it looks like an upside-down dagger—and I guess that's pretty much what it is. The cross is where our sin and our pain are turned upside down and the deadly point is buried in the ground and with it, *"all the bitterness and wrath and anger and wrangling and slander...."* [3] What's left is the image of a blunted dagger OR the shape of a man with outstretched arms, reminding us to *"be kind to one another, tenderhearted, forgiving one another, as God in Christ has forgiven you."* [4]

By now both Georges, the one who gave me life and the one who tried to take my life, have stood before their Maker.

I hope the same piercing miracle that touched my dad's soul touched George's heart as well before he died. I pray that each of them was welcomed into glory with the words, *"Well done, good and faithful servant."* [5]

The memento mounted under the inscribed plaque above my desk is a letter opener. It reminds me of the choice God has given us all. Each time I see it on the wall beside a sketch of my father, I ask the question, *Which George are you?* It's a good question for all of us to ask.

Which George are you?

14

HURRICANE VAN

And behold, the Lord passed by, and a great and strong wind rent the mountains, and broke in pieces the rocks before the Lord, but the Lord was not in the wind; and after the wind an earthquake, but the Lord was not in the earthquake; and after the earthquake a fire, but the Lord was not in the fire: and after the fire a still small voice.

I KINGS 19:11B–12 RSV

The children thought it hilarious that Grandpa Ed had forgotten to pack any underwear. Bennett was giggling harder than the others.

I finally realized that he thought I had said, "Grandpa forgot to WEAR any underwear!" I assured him that I was not yet that forgetful! We all piled in the van and headed to Target to purchase the above-mentioned unmentionables.

It was a long rainy weekend in Sacramento, and Grandma Linda and I had been entrusted with babysitting four of our grandchildren while their parents enjoyed a weekend getaway.

We had all sat indoors for hours going stir crazy from the constant drizzle that had held us captive inside since the weekend began. Compared to watching rain roll down the glass patio doors, a trip to Target, even for underwear, sounded like a thrilling change of pace. We were the first in a long line of customers when the cheerful greeter opened the door.

"Welcome to Target. May I help you find something?"

"UNDERWEAR! GRANPA ED FORGOT HIS UNDERWEAR!" shouted Bennett, age ten. The waiting gang of customers all chuckled—evidently the rainy weekend had left everyone longing for entertainment.

The reprieve from boredom was short-lived. Soon we were back at home in the family room. The rain beading on the glass patio doors was slowly giving us all *cabin fever*. We were huddled around a board game (aptly named; we were all *bored stiff*). We were supposed to be having fun but the game had long outlasted its ability to hypnotize us away from our dreary imprisonment.

As the game progressed, more humidity was building in the eyes of everyone but the impending contest winner. When the winner declared victory, the rest of the table disintegrated into a weeping cloudburst. It was time for an *emergency redirection*! Seizing the moment, I stood from my chair and shouted the first thing that came into my head—the only thing I could think of on short notice.

"Let's go storm chasing," I said.

It worked! The teary *downpour* in the children's eyes was instantly arrested. Their astonished faces peered at me in disbelief. Evidently storm chasing had never before been suggested by an adult in their home.

"Storm chasing," said the youngest, his forehead wrinkling as his eyebrows rose.

"What's storm chasing?"

Recalling the brief news segment I'd watched the night before (after the children were in bed), I shared my deep reservoir of expertise on the subject.

"It's when you get in the specially-equipped *Hurricane Van*, buckle up tight, and go chasing storms." (I left out the part about risking life and limb for an adrenaline rush. What I had in mind was a quiet drive around the block in the modest rainfall with the windshield wipers on.)

"But we don't have a *Hurricane Van*," said Hallie, age seven, with uncertainty in her voice.

I responded with all the authority of a grandpa who was a major-league hurricane hunter.

"All blue Dodge Caravans are equipped for hurricane duty. What color is yours?"

"BLUE!" they responded in wide-eyed unison.

"Quick then," I said.

"Put on your shoes; grab your coats—to the Hurricane Van!"

Grandma looked at me with a mystified gaze as the children turned hesitantly toward her. They were looking for one of two things—either final permission to *suit up*—OR a contradictory command based on Grandpa's lack of mental health.

The silence would have been deafening were it not for the sound of serious rain on the roof. Grandma was bored too. Her face softened into a knowing smile and she shouted to the children.

"Get your shoes and coats—to the Hurricane Van!"

The children raced for their upstairs rooms like firefighters at the sound of the alarm. There was a momentary logjam at the first step, then the drumming of sock-covered feet ascending the carpeted steps. Tyler, the youngest, paused for a moment at the bottom of the stairs and looked back. Grandma and I peered at him as he hesitated. Then, like a general on horseback, he shouted ahead to the charging troops.

"To the Hurricane Van"—melt-down averted, mission (temporarily) accomplished!

"Now what?" said Grandma after they had left the room.

"Relax," I said, "I've got this!"

The children spanned some of life's most magical ages. Tyler, age four, was totally immersed in the adventure as absolute reality. Hallie and Bennett (the *middles*) knew this was a spoof but the authority in our adult voices left a question as to whether there was something more than child's play in this adventure. Royce, age twelve, joined in the fantasy for the sheer joy of amusing the little ones and the hope of breaking free of our rainy day detention.

We piled into the Dodge Caravan and I turned the radio on—and off again quickly! I cupped my hand and spoke into it as though it was a radio transmitter.

"Storm Tracker Central, do you read?" (I imitated the sound of crackling interference between the phrases.)

"This is *Danger Team Mobile* ready to launch. Our coordinates are one, two, *niner* by four, five Sacramento … requesting permission."

Hurricane Control came back on the radio. They gave us the *go ahead* in a garbled voice that sounded strangely like my own.

"Pre takeoff checklist!" I barked to the children.

"Coats on?"

"Coats on," they excitedly repeated.

"Shoes tied?"

"Shoes tied," they echoed.

"Ashtrays empty?" They flicked the little chrome trap doors near their seats.

Giggling, Tyler spoke, "Hey! There's old chewing gum in mine."

"Never mind that now," I answered, "We're too close to takeoff; we'll have to jettison it later. Brace for launch."

The *Hurricane Van*, still in the garage, roared its mighty four-cylinder engine as I buckled myself into the *captain's chair*.

My cautious copilot put her hand on mine, "Careful, Grandpa; not too fast."

"Roger that," I reassured her, making eye contact with a wink.

As we backed out of the garage, I saw the children's faces in the rearview mirror; their eyes, the size of saucers, were beaming with excitement. Raindrops rolling down the windshield of a Hurricane Van are spectacular compared to raindrops rolling down glass patio doors.

My voice boomed confidence as I buckled into the *captain's chair* behind the wheel. Now even I was beginning to believe in the special powers of the blue Dodge Hurricane Van.

"Hold on tight; I'm going to have to use hyperdrive to cut through this weather."

Launching from our cul-de-sac, I echoed our progress to the

crew: "Five miles per hour.... Ten miles per hour.... Fifteen miles per hour.... Don't give in to the G-forces—Try to stay conscious."

Rolling down the highway, Grandma and I explained to the children how you can see a storm front approaching by looking for a dark gray veil in the distance. They began peering out the windows in anticipation.

"I see it," shouted Royce, "It's over there, toward the hills."

He had seen what Grandma and I had already spotted: a curtain of ominous gray was advancing on us from the distance.

"Grandma, set our course for those hills."

I nodded toward the radio buttons. She rolled her eyes and punched at the radio buttons—accidentally activating a CD of *the Backstreet Boys* for a millisecond before engaging the *storm tracker*.

"Perfect!" I said, "Hold the course right there."

As we sped along the open road, the cross-wind tested my hands on the steering wheel and the van swerved slightly. No one was thinking about board games now, *we weren't in Kansas anymore*—this was beginning to be a real storm!

Bennett shouted over the clamor of the rain beating on the van's roof, "Wow, look at the rain—it's flying sideways!"

As the wind and rain buffeted the van, I began to think thoughts to myself that I dared not share with the kids—or Grandma. Thoughts like; *Wow, this really is a storm. I wonder if we should have stayed at home.* I glanced at the rearview mirror to see the children in the seats behind me. Their saucer-sized eyes had widened to dinner plates—Grandma's looked more like serving platters.

About twenty Black Angus huddled in the open against an old wire fence at the crest of the hill. They had turned their backs to the wind which was now blowing the rain at them with the force of a Nor'easter. Seeking to avoid panic in my troops, I doubled down with commanding confidence and said, "Look, that herd of cows over there doesn't seem to mind a little sideways rain!" The words no sooner cleared my lips than the cows suddenly *lost their cool* and bolted furiously for the barn! The rain had turned to hail, and ice chunks the size of walnuts were now hammering both the herd AND the *Hurricane Van*. I'm not sure I have ever seen a cow derby before, but there they were, running from the hail like thoroughbreds straining for the finish line. The children held their breath in wonder at the raging deluge. I tried to avoid direct eye contact with Grandma!

The storm grew louder and louder. We attempted yelling to each other but the thundering clatter on the metal roof silenced our straining voices. Grandma looked at me; her penetrating gaze seemed to say, *Okay, 'Ace,' you got us into this; you'd better get us out!* Her inaudible message was interrupted as a car in front of us slowly slid off the slick road and landed quietly in a shallow ditch before our eyes. In the next mile we saw two cars that had involuntarily *parked* in the same way. The road wreckage only punctuated the excitement for the kids—not so much for Grandma! I lightly pumped the brake to slow down.

Even I, *a seasoned hurricane hunter*, became a little nervous at the pounding weather around us. It would be difficult to explain hail holes in the van to the children's parents. I silently wondered if Dodge Caravan windshields were tested as *hail shields*.

As a leader I knew I had to keep hope alive; I shouted at the top of my lungs (though I don't know if anyone heard me), "We're going to go airborne to get out of this ground turbulence. Don't be frightened; when you can't feel the road rumble under us, it means we've flown into the eye of the hurricane!" With little visibility from the pounding deluge, I pulled to the side of the country road and braked to a slow safe stop.

"We'll be safe here until the storm lets up!" The storm was so loud it was as if I had not spoken. We sat wordless, gaping at the banging, bouncing ice as though all the angels of heaven were playing table tennis at once and we were the table. Grandma looked at me not knowing whether to laugh, cry, or scream. It was time for another *emergency redirection!*

As the storm hit a lull, I shouted in comic relief, "Grandma, get the snack cart out and serve the soft drinks and pretzels." No one laughed!

"Soft drinks and pretzels?" Tyler repeated my words hopefully.

"I have a better idea," I said. "When the weather clears, let's see if we can set this thing down near a McDonalds. This hail is making me hungry for soft-serve ice cream!"

We sat in quiet anticipation as the thundering storm slowly dissipated. Finally, I could see the road well enough to drive again. We slid around on the muddy soft shoulder for a few seconds before the tires took hold of the pavement. The kids all thought this was part of the fun—I was relieved when we found traction on the highway again.

Once we had landed safely at McDonalds, I inspected "Danger Team Mobile" for damage—there was none. Blue *Hurricane Vans* are evidently clobberproof!

Like the weather, the adrenaline had now dissipated and the relief had left us all silly. Sitting at a table with our ice cream cones, we retold our storm adventures to one another until the kids were laughing hysterically. The fun was contagious; two other tables of total strangers began laughing as well. None of us were exactly sure about what was so funny!

That night in the family room we lay side-by-side on the floor like dominos. We interlocked our arms and retold the story of our day with giggles as we remembered the galloping cows, the sliding cars, and the deafening hail. We recalled how you could actually see the curtain of gray rain in the distance before it started falling on you. Finally, we all lay there once again in the imagined eye of the hurricane and we prayed together. Each one genuinely thanked God for one thing... stampeding race cows... the taste of sweet ice cream... the invisible protection that had surrounded us in the van.

An hour later Grandma and I peeked in at our four sleeping pilgrims who had finally reached their destination. They slept sound and serene in stark contrast to the thunderous excitement and uncontrollable hilarity we'd experienced earlier. All the commotion of creation had rumbled, blown, and raged around us that day—yet this is the moment I remember most—watching them sleep peacefully in their beds. God had safely surrounded us in riotous rainfall and avalanching laughter; God was now surrounding us in the silent crescendo of His whisper-soft presence. The ancients feared the gods and worshiped wind, earthquake, and fire but He is not these things—He is a *still small voice.*[1] His is the voice that whispers to us in the bedroom of a sleeping child. It is one and the same voice, powerful enough to create everything there is from nothing, yet personal enough to whisper to you and me in the silence.[2]

Many of life's most enduring memories come camouflaged. We never know which moments will become lifetime treasures until our minds uncover them years, even decades later. The truth is that any day can become extraordinary and any circumstance magnificent because, as Elijah learned, we never climb a mountain or descend to a valley alone. He puts his hand upon us and tells us to buckle up, take the wheel, and, if necessary, *make it up as we go along.* His promise is that something good will come out of every storm. Our job is to keep a strong hand on the wheel each day and to listen quietly for His whisper every night.

15

GRANDMA'S COOKIE JAR

But we have this treasure in clay jars, so that it may be made clear that this extraordinary power belongs to God and does not come from us.

II CORINTHIANS 4:7

My mother gave me a trophy case of antique glassware before she passed on. Surprisingly, it's a common clay cookie jar that's far more precious to me today. The classic glassware crafted by my grandfather's company 150 years ago sits in a corner hutch in our living room. Grandma Carol's cookie jar always sat on her kitchen counter. I never owned it, but for special reasons I'll always remember it.

It was a round-bellied, thin-necked jar, powder blue in color with a bright gold top notch and matching gold handles. It certainly wasn't real gold. Some of my mother's crystal has contours that are gilded with real gold leaf—you can tell the difference. The gold on the cookie jar was just glossy paint but that's not what made it important. The importance of the cookie jar is that it was always full! I guess that's why I remember the cookie jar at all—because of the love Grandma Carol baked into it. I never remember a time when she knew we were coming to visit that she didn't bake snicker doodles or oatmeal raisin cookies or my favorite, chocolate chip.

I visited Grandma Carol over many ages and stages in her life. In fact, I followed her over forty years to five different dwellings that she called home. All the homes were different but one thing was always the same. That familiar blue and gold cookie jar always sat under the cupboard on the kitchen counter not far from the table where we would sit, laugh, and drink tea and, of course, eat cookies.

I first knew Grandma Carol as a Sunday school teacher. She taught third grade along with my mother at our church. Little did I know then that she would one day become my mother-in-law and "Grandma Carol" to my children.

Grandma's cookie jar acquired some dings and lost some gloss over the years. One of its golden handles came off one day due to the eagerness of a grandchild to get at the good stuff inside. One of Grandma Carol's daughters came to the rescue with glue and acrylic paint to restore its faded glory. She did a pretty good job, good enough for the jar to be presentable in public, though not quite with the same splendor of its youth. It didn't really matter to us. When we arrived hungry from the drive to Grandma's house, we didn't care what the outside of the jar looked like, we wondered what the surprise would be on the inside. We were never disappointed.

Grandma Carol's girls were fond of telling cookie jar stories from their past. They recalled story after story of how they would try to sneak a cookie and put the ceramic lid back on without being discovered. Grandma's ears were tuned to the sound of ceramic; no matter how hard they tried, they never got away with it. Later their children, her grandchildren, were given complete access to the jar at every visit. As Grandma ripened, she got better at saying yes. She said no only when rarely necessary.

Both Grandma and her cookie jar came from humble beginnings. She had picked the cookie jar up at a thrift store or garage sale long ago—she couldn't remember when. She herself had come from a little-known farming community in Wyoming called Chugwater, population 212. Neither Grandma nor her cookie jar gave the slightest pretense of self-importance.

Like her cookie jar, Grandma Carol also lost some gloss and acquired some dings over the years. According to her, in her early years she'd been "a handful" for her parents. She'd run away from home, done some things she regretted, and married very young. She struggled through a second marriage and in time renewed her faith in God. That combination of tough times and renewed trust rounded her rough edges and softened her stubborn will.

She was always quick to admit that she was still a work in progress. I guess it's kind of like learning to bake cookies. You burn several batches before you get to the place where they turn out scrumptious *almost* every time. There are so many things to get right or wrong in cookie baking—and life: the right ingredients, the right mix, the right timing, following the tried-and-true recipe. Trial and error is often what it takes to finally begin to get it right—every time you get burned, you learn what NOT to do the next time. Adding a little love to your ingredients is essential. In the end, by paying attention, Grandma Carol got the recipe down pretty good. To her credit, even in her *perfection*, she knew she was not beyond spoiling any given batch on any given day if she failed to be attentive! The way she told it, a young woman who'd been pretty focused on the superficial outer person began, with God's help, to focus more on what was inside. She returned to teaching Sunday school as she had done in her youth, and she settled down to raise her children. When her own children were grown, after her second divorce, she met Grandpa Keith, and he was attracted to the woman she had become. In fact, it was her example that led him to a deeper faith and a renewed joy in serving others.

Grandma Carol and Keith had a spacious home with a player piano, an inviting patio, and a large swimming pool. They remembered how lonely they had been before they met each other, especially on Sunday afternoons when families seemed more likely to be together. It wasn't long before they were opening their home every Sunday to dozens of single people from their church who would come to pump the player piano and sing and swim in the pool. Every Sunday was a potluck dinner and—you guessed it—Grandma Carol would bake cookies for their guests.

When the people who came to the potluck talked to her about their problems, she was not judgmental; she'd had lots of problems herself. They would talk and she would listen and then she would invite them to come again later in the week for a more private conversation, and for tea and cookies. With nothing but tea and cookies and a table between them, she would listen and then she would pray for them. The meeting would always end with a hug and an invitation back for more cookies another time.

Even when Grandma Carol got sick and nerve damage affected her smile, she made people feel like she was smiling at them with her warm welcome, the tone of her voice, and her generous hospitality!

The last time I saw Grandma Carol she was in an assisted-living home for people who struggled with memory loss. She didn't remember my name but she recognized me as a friend, not a stranger. By God's grace, in the end there was none of that rebellious young woman fighting for her rights, there was only the sweet welcome of Jesus within her and, oh yes—there was an offer of tea and cookies.

She didn't realize that she could no longer be trusted with the fire to heat the water or bake the cookie dough. Her oven and stove top had been disconnected for her own safety. I think it was the only time I declined one of her cookies because I didn't want her to go through the distress of searching for cookies that I knew she didn't have.

I walked away from Grandma Carol's door for the last time that day as *full* as I had ever been before. In the best sense the sweetness was still there, the warm greeting of the now crooked yet unmistakably welcoming smile, the hug, the offer to sit and talk. We talked and talked. The conversation would have made little sense to an outsider, but there was laughter and love in her eyes. We reached out our hands to one another and held them as we prayed. At the end of the prayer was her loud "Amen!" It means "So be it!" or "Thy will be done!"

Over a lifetime, I believe, Jesus baked Himself into Grandma Carol as surely as she had baked herself into ten thousand cookies and shared them with others. When she passed into the arms of God and the day came for the celebration of her life, I asked the several hundred who had gathered, "How many of you have tasted one of Grandma Carol's great cookies?" Nearly every hand in the packed sanctuary went up!

I grin whenever I think of Grandma Carol. She wasn't perfect, but I think she learned some good lessons in life and used them to be a blessing to a lot of people. When I think of that powder blue cookie jar with the bright gold top notch, I smile again. It reminds me that while we may not all have a cookie jar—with God's help, our real purpose is to BE a cookie jar.

16

THE BEST CHRISTMAS
PRESENT EVER

No matter how deep the stain of your sins,
    I can take it out and make you as clean as freshly
fallen snow.

ISAIAH 1:18 TLB

I don't think of myself as a *bad* person. I don't think of myself as a *good* person either. I try to avoid scoring my performance for purposes of flogging or framing. In the end, I know I'm not the one who gets to judge. The *Ultimate Umpire* pays no attention to either the crowd or to the batter's self-serving bias; *He just calls it as he sees it*! We don't get to fill out our own report cards. If we did, we'd always get caught leaning in our own favor.

The truth is most of us think of ourselves as better than the next guy. Oh, maybe not better than Mother Teresa or Albert Schweitzer but certainly better than our sweetheart's old boyfriend or that annoying neighbor with the barking dog. When a person says, "I'm a good person," they are usually sifting through the competition carefully to exclude Teresa and Albert from the running. Do you really think that Hitler and Mussolini actually thought of themselves as "bad people?"

Of course, there are some people who always think of themselves as failures, but for most of us the truth is that sometimes we do well and sometimes we mess up. We're *im*-perfect. We may aim for *dead center* but often we end up outside the *bull's-eye*.

It was nearing the Christmas of 1962 and my second (and briefest) girlfriend was Sherry Blake. Sherry had made the cheerleading squad at the high school across town. I never dated a cheerleader in my own high school but from across town I guess I looked better! I also looked better in my dad's 1960 Chevy coupe which I managed to borrow for important dates. I was a senior, Sherry was a sophomore, I had a cool car—I think the car helped a lot!

This was back in the days when there were no seat belts in cars and no consoles separated you from your date. I remember what a thrill it was to pick Sherry up and have her slide over into the middle of the seat beside me. If you lived in that era, you know the feeling

I'm talking about; it wasn't static electricity from the car seat, but it was *electricity!* What a thrill it was to sit behind the steering wheel just inches away from a bubble-gum scented, rock 'n' roll-loving, real live pedal-pusher-wearing female. Little could compare to rolling away on a Saturday night for several hours of uninterrupted parental absence.

Unfortunately, just before Christmas, Sherry dumped me for a pitcher on her school's baseball team.

I never saw the *changeup* coming. His parents had bought him his very own jalopy. It was some old *bucket of bolts* but it was completely his—what a spoiled jerk! He had to be pampered beyond repair to have his "mommy" and "daddy" buy him his own car in high school! But enough about him, let's talk about ME some more!

Sherry didn't tell me about our breakup; *I heard it through the grapevine.* She just stopped returning my calls and then my friends broke the news. I was heartbroken.

A few weeks later, while the wound was still bleeding, Frankie Valli and the Four Seasons scored their first No. 1 hit, "Sherry Baby."[1] I couldn't drive anywhere without being ambushed by the original Jersey Boys on my favorite radio station. That song is still on my iTunes playlist for those melancholy times when I just DON'T WANT to feel better!

By Christmas *rigor mortis* had finally set in; my heart was numb. The long drives with Sherry snuggling beside me in the front seat were over. The only thing that felt good to me was feeling bad. For me and Elvis it was a "Blue Christmas."[2] I was a senior in high school with a driver's license and no female to drive anywhere except my mother.

Mom had tried once as a teenager to take her driving test in the dead of winter. It had been a snowy day in Pennsylvania. The roads were icy and she skidded on the pavement and failed the test. Uncharacteristically, she never went back.

Mom was very happy that I could drive. Often, I would drive Dad to work in the family car and then run my mother around town on errands picking Dad up after his shift. Our town was small, and at sixteen I loved being behind the wheel, even if it was my mom who was riding *shotgun.*

I still remember how commonplace Christmas morning felt to me that year. The gifts seemed fewer than usual and less exciting. When all the packages had been opened, Mom suggested we go into the backyard for a family picture.

It felt a little odd to be huddling under a lemon tree in the center of the yard for a family picture but we all lined up dutifully under the branches as directed. Mom stood beside me and annoyingly kept pushing me into a low-hanging branch. Finally, I bumped into a gift tag that was attached like an ornament to the tree. It read, "Merry Christmas Eddie—follow the string." The string looped over the tree branches and led across our yard into our neighbor's garage. I followed the string as my heart began to pound. I pushed open the door and there it was—my first car! It was a brand-new 1963, bright-white, two-door Dodge Dart. I had no idea it was coming. It was a complete surprise!

I took my first test drive. It had everything, *three-on-the-tree* (standard transmission with the gear shift on the column), AM radio, a bright red interior, and a sparkling-white chassis with a thin red pin stripe from taillight to headlight.

I drove home with incredible pride and confidence—so much confidence—that I immediately called Sherry to see if she'd like to take a drive that night! I guess I thought of her as a woman of shallow substance who might be coaxed away from *Cy Young* by a guy who owned his own NEW car! She was! She said, "Yes!"

Later that night I picked her up and we went for the ride. Strangely, our reunion wasn't as fun as I'd thought it would be. I think as we drove I discovered it wasn't so much that I loved the girl who dropped me; it's that I hated the feeling of getting dumped! Looking back on the "date," it felt less like a revived romance and more like I'd just hit a homer off my crosstown rival—it felt good, but it didn't feel right. I think that was the only time I didn't walk a girl back to her front steps. As I closed the passenger door and drove away, I began to realize that I wasn't looking for love: it was just my bruised ego that was driving me to petty revenge. I never called her again. Of course to be fair she never called me either. I think I only saw Sherry once after that; we didn't speak.

I had a new love now, a more dependable one with red racing stripes. I cared for my new love like it was a rare Rolls Royce. It was the whitest white I had ever seen. I came to notice that whenever I pulled up next to another white car the other car's brilliance was compromised. Every other white car faded next to my Dart's polished purity. Only once do I remember any disappointment associated with that dazzling Dodge. It was on a dry, crisp winter day when I drove to the mountains and parked the car next to the cabin in which I was to stay. The window of my bedroom looked out on the driveway so I could keep an eye on my new treasure. I woke the next morning to a brilliant sunrise and a thick layer of blinding snow blanketing everything. In the breathless quiet, all was covered in two inches of white powder; the porch railings, the driveway, even the trash cans next to my car glistened with snow.

As I stared at the spotless purity that crested the heaven-facing surfaces of my car, I became aware of a shocking blemish. Centimeters beneath the glimmering snow that covered my pride and joy were the naked GRAY side panels of my Dodge—though freshly polished, my Dart looked dull and lifeless in contrast to the new-fallen snow! In the midst of the radiant white landscape, my car looked the color of soiled cement. I'd never seen its sparkling grandeur look so glum. Another coat of polish would have only proved its hopeless condition. Under the thick layer of new-fallen snow, my car was not as pure as I had imagined.

Sometimes I've wondered if I'm really a good guy worthy of the lavish gifts in life that I have been given or whether I'm just a spoiled selfish egotist who wants the cool car, the pretty girl, and to get even with anyone who hurts me. I've come to believe that this dual diagnosis IS who I am. The Bible says this diagnosis is true of all of us and the only effective cure is to believe in Christmas.

No matter how good we are, we are not perfect and no matter how bad we are, we are not worthless to God. Intuitively, we know this is true and so we preoccupy ourselves with polishing our various shades of gray in hopes of shining a little brighter than average.

Polishing my gray Dart wouldn't have made it whiter than snow and polishing our best behavior doesn't make us perfect. Instead, like a comforter of new-fallen snow, God lays his quilt of purity upon us from on high. The innocent blood of Jesus both cleanses and covers us. If we stand silent in his grace long enough to let this *snow* cover us, it hides both our sins and our best attempts to be lovable.

When the Father looks at us, He sees the perfection of Jesus—He wraps us in it! He wraps us in it as surely as Mary *"wrapped him; in swaddling clothes, and laid him in a manger."*[3] My white Dodge Dart was not the best Christmas present ever—but it reminds me of the One who is.

In Memory of your bravery
The Unnamed Resident debacle
Apartment 22

END NOTES

Table of Contents:

1. "God loves each one of us...." This is a paraphrase from Saint Augustine: "You are good and all-powerful, caring for each one of us as though the only one in your care." Augustine, *Confessions,* trans. Henry Chadwick (Oxford: Oxford University Press, 2009,) 3.11.19, p. 50.
2. *"Confession is good...."* Popularly considered to be an old Scottish proverb. No source found.
3. I Peter 4:8b

Author's Note:

1. *"Truth is stranger...."* This old adage is perhaps paraphrased from Lord Byron's satirical poem *Don Juan,* 1823: "Tis strange – but true; for truth is always strange; Stranger than fiction...."

Chapter 1. Marzipan Bananas:

1. Exodus 20:4a (KJV)
2. Genesis 3:6

Chapter 2. One-Eyed Teddy:

1. Genesis 1:31
2. Romans 5:8

Chapter 3. Packards and Pop Guns:

1. Psalm 139:18b (RSV)

Chapter 4. Trouble at the Ball Cupboard:

1. Genesis 25:26 Footnote in NLT "Jacob sounds like the Hebrew words for "heel" and "deceiver."
2. Genesis 32:28 (Msg)

Chapter 5. Home before Dark:

1. Romans 8:39 NLT

Chapter 8. Fire on the Hill:

1. Matthew 5:14a

Chapter 10. Angels among Us:

1. Matthew 7:12 NIV
2. Hebrews 13:2

Chapter 11. The Cheer of the Cloud:

1. Hebrews 12:1

Chapter 12. Keeping the Birds from Their Mission:

1. *The Birds,* 1963 film produced and directed by Alfred J. Hitchcock
2. Widely attributed to Martin Luther but no direct source was found.

Chapter 13. Unrest in the Rest Home:

1. Matthew 25:21 KJV
2. Luke 23:34
3. Ephesians 4:31
4. Ephesians 4:32
5. Matthew 25:21 KJV

Chapter 14. Hurricane Van:

1. I Kings 19:12 RSV
2. John 1:1–5 indicates that God created the world, entered our

world in the person of Jesus, and still shines in the darkness though the "Word."

Chapter 16. The Best Christmas Present Ever:

1. Written by Bob Gaudio and recorded by the Four Seasons, Released August 1962, Vee-Jay Records
2. Written by Billy Hayes and Jay W. Johnson and recorded by Elvis Presley, Released November 9, 1964, RCA Victor
3. Luke 2:7 KJV

CPSIA information can be obtained
at www.ICGtesting.com
Printed in the USA
LVHW09s0427200918
590707LV00001B/1/P